AN URGENT TASK:

WHAT BISHOPS AND PRIESTS SAY ABOUT RELIGIOUS EDUCATION PROGRAMS

by
J. Stephen O'Brien

published by

National Catholic
Educational Association

TABLE OF CONTENTS

PREFACE

Bishops and priests have substantial power and influence over what happens in the daily life of the church, including its educational ministry. Therefore, it is very important to know what their vision is for parish religious education. Even though they are zealous for the work of the Lord, zeal alone is not enough to ensure effective catechesis. For church education to be effective, the bishops and priests need to exercise leadership, articulate vision, and be persistent. This study is a modest attempt to find out how the bishops and priests view their mission in religious education.

In the final chapter of this book, I have tried to be cautious about drawing conclusions from the data. I presume that the reader is capable of arriving at her or his own conclusions. However, in the "Reflections" section of that chapter, I have concentrated on the lack of data on catechesis available to the church in the United States. These reflections flow from the data compiled here, but are not limited to that data.

I applaud all of the people in parish religious education programs who work so diligently and enthusiastically to proclaim the Good News of Jesus in a culture that often has a different focus. May they not have to wait for heaven for their reward!

I would like to thank publicly the people who made this study possible: the generous bishops and priests who took the time to answer the questionnaire; Archbishop John Roach for his support; Elaine McCarron, SCN, Stephen M. Colecchi, Rev. John Unger, Ann Lacour, MSC, Susanne Hofweber, OP, Mary Elizabeth Hogan and 35 priests from the Diocese of Richmond for invaluable help in developing the questionnaire; Dr. Mary M. Bender for patient technical assistance.

Margaret C. McBrien, Lourdes Sheehan, RSM, Wayne Smith, Robert W. Meaney, Rev. Christopher Smith, Edith Prendergast, RSC, Joan E. Brady, Sharon Ford, RSM, Janet E. Kayser, Sylvia Marotta, Karen Murphy, Marietta Sharkey, OSF, Anne Marie Smith, OSF, Kathryn Ann Connelly, SC, and Roberta Schmidt, CSJ, for critically reading the manuscript and for not being hesitant in their comments.

I am also grateful to Mary V. Barnes for mailing questionnaires, putting in data, and typing tables and to Lorie Catsos for typing the original draft of the manuscript.

Stephen O'Brien
January, 1989

CHAPTER 1:
A PROFILE OF UNITED STATES BISHOPS AND PRIESTS

Catechesis and "Pastors of Souls"

The 1983 Code of Canon Law, the universal law of the Catholic Church, views catechesis as a pastoral activity, a part of the ministry of the word. Because catechesis is a very broad term, some people make a distinction between catechesis and religious education. In this contemporary view, catechesis is the umbrella concept and religious education describes the more formal catechetical endeavors of the church for adults, youth and children (O'Brien, 1987a, pp. 7-8). For the purposes of this study, the term used is parish religious education program. It includes formal parish catechetical programs for all ages, but unless otherwise stated excludes Catholic schools.

The Code clearly places the responsibility for catechesis with bishops and pastors of parishes. Canon 773 states:

> There is a proper and serious duty, especially on the part of pastors of souls [bishops and pastors], to provide for the catechesis of the Christian people so that the faith of the faithful becomes living, explicit and productive through formation in doctrine and the experience of Christian living.

In Canon 776, the Code explicitly informs the pastor of his duties:

> In virtue of his office the pastor is bound to provide for the catechetical formation of adults, young people and children , to which end he is to employ the services of the clerics attached to the parish, members of institutes of consecrated life . . . and lay members of the Christian faithful, above all catechists; all of these are not to refuse to furnish their services willingly unless they are legitimately impeded. The pastor is to promote and foster the role of parents in the family catechesis . . . (Canon 776).

The National Catechetical Directory, *Sharing the Light of Faith* (1979) (NCD) also acknowledges the responsibility of the pastor in the catechetical ministry of the church; and it offers specific guidelines on how the pastor can fulfill those responsibilities. Pastors are called "a source of leadership, cooperation, and support for all involved in this ministry." Their catechetical functions are listed as "encouraging catechists, praying with them, teaching and learning with them, supporting them." Further, pastors are called to participate in planning, catechizing, preaching, and celebrating the sacraments as a central point of the catechesis of the community (#217).

Pastors do not carry the responsibility of catechesis alone. As the NCD states:

> The pastor is primarily responsible for seeing to it that the catechetical needs, goals, and priorities of the parish are identified, articulated, and met. In planning and carrying out the catechetical ministry, he works with his priests associates, parish council, board of education or analogous body, directors and coordinators, principals, teachers, parents, and others. He respects the organizational principles mentioned [here] and attempts to make as much use as possible of team ministry in catechetical efforts (#217)

Thus catechetical ministry works best when there is cooperation and collaboration.

Background Data

Some of the data given here has been previously reported in *Mixed Messages* (O'Brien, 1987b). However, there is new information regarding bishops' and priests' relationships to parish catechetical programs.

The questionnaire consisted of 53 statements that focused on the areas of the purpose, effectiveness and administration of parish religious education programs. Bishops and priests indicated their agreement or disagreement with the statements on a four point scale from strongly agree to strongly disagree. The statements themselves were developed from church documents, the findings of other studies, and from the conventional wisdom of people in the church (See Appendix B).

Because of their different sources, the statements are not always consistent with one another. For example, one statement proposed that the purpose of religious education for children is the effects it has on adults who are connected with the program. Another indicated that the purpose is to help people grow in faith into mature adulthood. The purpose of this study was not only to see how much bishops and priests agreed with church documents, but also how much they have accepted the results of other research and conventional wisdom.

At the time of the survey, there were 276 active Roman Catholic bishops in the United States. All were sent a copy of the questionnaire; 200 or 73 percent responded. According to *The Official Catholic Directory*, there were 38,839 priests in parish ministry. A random sample of 655 received the questionnaire; 47 percent responded. Their responses were validated by contacting a random sample of the priests who had not responded. (For more information on the research methodology, see Appendix A.)

Age and Role

When the survey was taken, the average age of an active bishop in the United States was 60. He had been ordained a priest for 35 years and a bishop for 12. Over 68 percent of the bishops were between the ages of 52 and 68; 75 percent were over the age of 56 (Table 1). Of those bishops who responded, 71 percent were diocesan bishops; 27 percent were auxiliaries and 2 percent were retired (Table C1, Appendix C).

The average priest who answered the questionnaire was 52 years old and had been ordained 25 years. Over 68 percent of the priests were between the ages of 39 and 65; 46 percent were over the age of 56 (Table 1).

The average bishop was ordained at age 25, but the average priest who answered

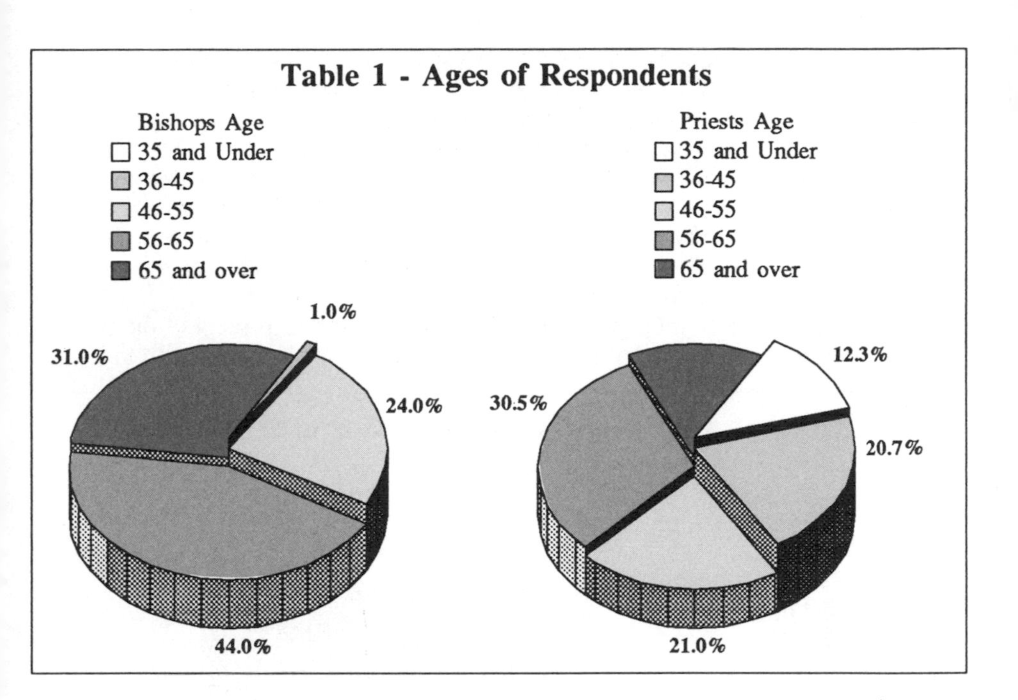
Table 1 - Ages of Respondents
Bishops Age
35 and Under
36-45
46-55
56-65
65 and over
Priests Age
35 and Under
36-45
46-55
56-65
65 and over
1.0%
31.0%
24.0%
44.0%
12.3%
30.5%
20.7%
21.0%

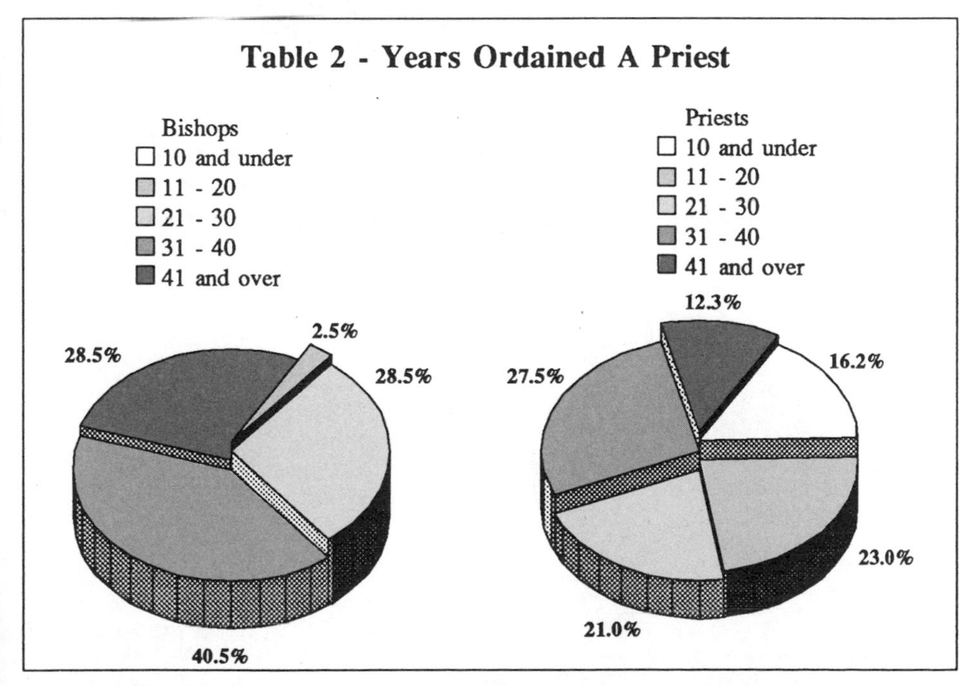
Table 2 - Years Ordained A Priest
Bishops
10 and under
11 - 20
21 - 30
31 - 40
41 and over
Priests
10 and under
11 - 20
21 - 30
31 - 40
41 and over
2.5%
28.5%
28.5%
40.5%
12.3%
27.5%
16.2%
23.0%
21.0%

the questionnaire was ordained at age 27. This result reflects the recent trend of men entering the seminary after several years in the work place (Table 2).

Most of the priests who answered the questionnaire, 59 percent, were pastors (48 percent of those who received the questionnaire were pastors); 22 percent were associates; 3 percent were involved in team ministry; and 16 percent said that they were primarily involved in non-parish ministry. The presumption is that the priests in this latter group do other work, but are assigned as part-time associates in parishes. Slightly less than 25 percent of the priests reported that they are members of religious communities (Table C1, Appendix C).

Although members of religious communities represented 25 percent of the priests, they included 56 percent of those who were primarily involved in non-parish ministry.

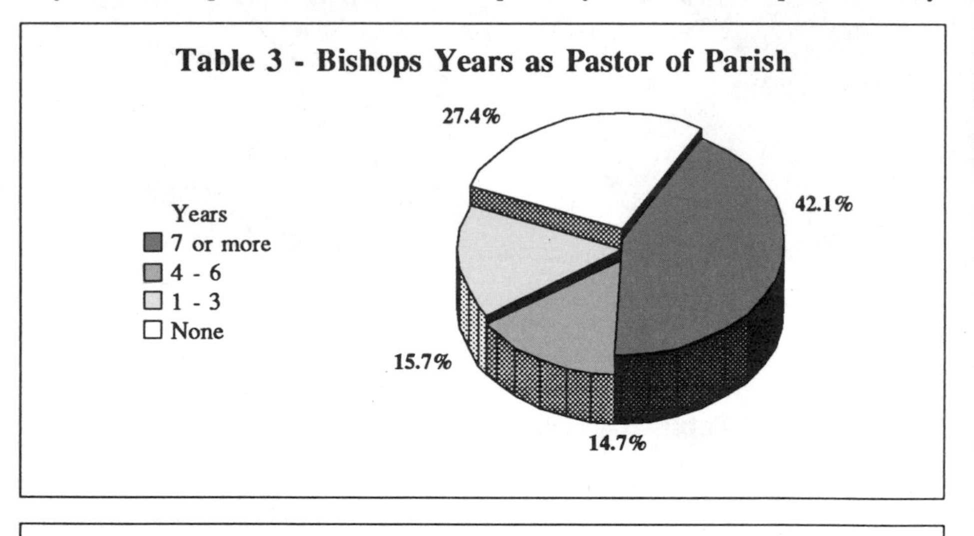

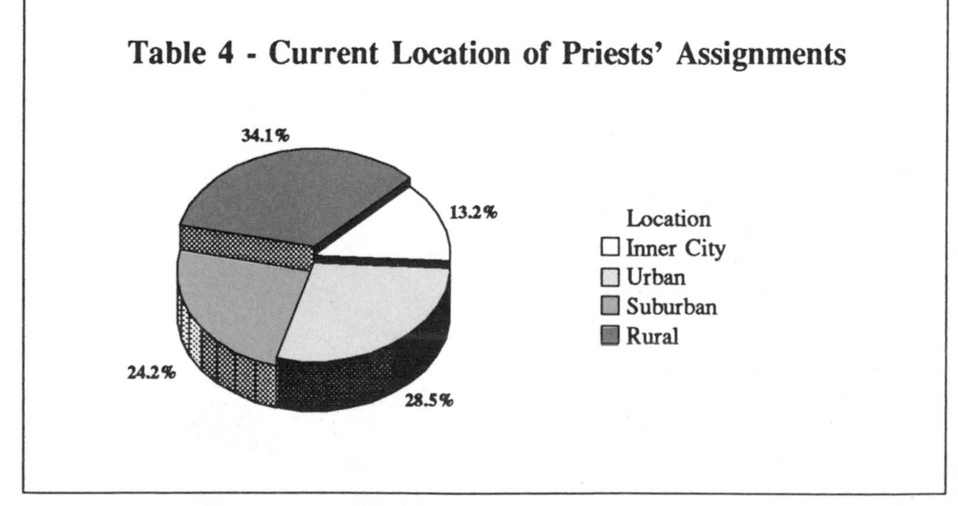

Members of religious communities represented 8 percent of the pastors, 20 percent of the associates, and 20 percent of those involved in team ministry (Table C2, Appendix C).

Table 3 shows the number of years that bishops have been pastors of parishes. Almost 73 percent of the bishops have been a pastor of a parish, with 42 percent having been a pastor for seven years or more.

Location and Ministry

In terms of the location of their ministry, 34 percent of the priests who responded work in rural areas of the country and 66 percent work in or near cities (Table 4). As has been reported previously, and as Table 5 indicates, 84 percent of the bishops and 83 percent of the priests attended Catholic elementary schools; and 88 percent of the bishops and 82 percent of the priests attended Catholic secondary schools.

The involvement with Catholic schools continued after ordination; 94 percent of the bishops and 91 percent of the priests have served in a parish with a school (Table 6). As might be expected, older bishops and priests have spent more time in parishes with schools than their younger colleagues (Table C3, Appendix C). A relatively large percentage of bishops (42%) and priests (43%) have been full-time administrators or teachers in a Catholic school. However, full-time involvement by priests has decreased substantially in recent years (Table C4, Appendix C).

More relevant to this study, 52 percent of the bishops and 63 percent of the priests said that they had been moderators or directors of a parish religious education program. The exact job description for those roles is not evident, but the response does show close connections and interest between many of the clergy and parish religious education programs.

As Table 7 indicates, 28 percent of the bishops and 26 percent of the priests attended a parish religious education program for at least a part of their religious education. Regionally, New England with 48 percent had the highest percentage of priests attending parish religious education programs; the Great Lakes and the Plains states had the least with 17 percent (Tables C5 and C6, Appendix C).

RCIA

Although only part of the *Rite of Christian Initiation of Adults* is catechetical, there was an additional question concerning its implementation. Many religious educators coordinated the RCIA when it was first introduced and many continue to do so today.

When the bishops were asked if, in general, the parishes in their dioceses had implemented the RCIA, 77 percent responded that they had. When the priests were asked if their parishes had implemented the RCIA, 59 percent responded that they had. Bishops probably have a more optimistic picture about parish involvement in the RCIA than seems to be the case.

With only 43 percent responding affirmatively, New England and the Mideast had the lowest percentage of parishes that had implemented the RCIA. The New England bishops were aware that there is a relatively low implementation rate in their area of the country. The bishops in the Mideast were not as aware of the role of the RCIA in parishes in their dioceses, since 71 percent reported general implementation

Table 5 - Catholic School Education

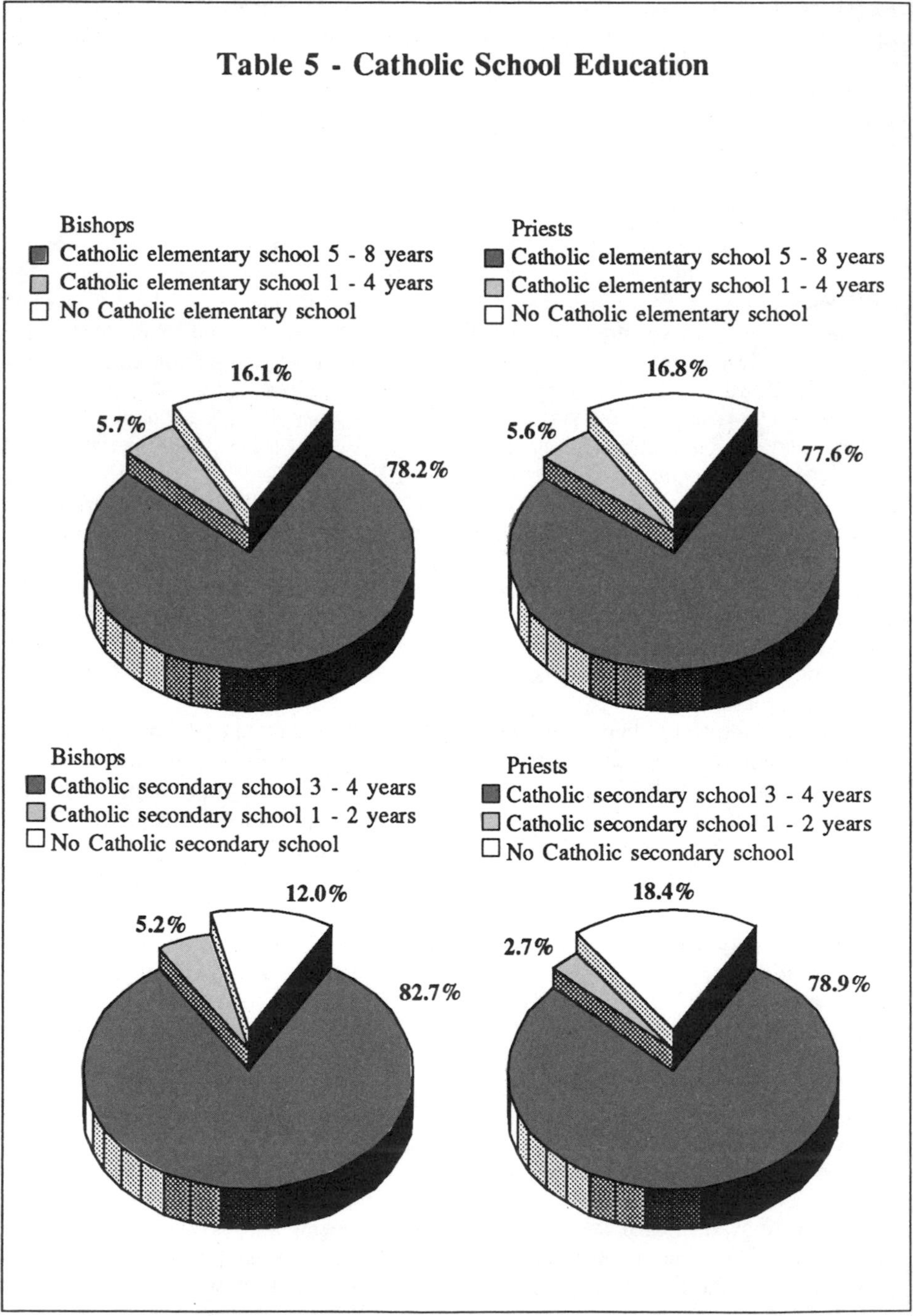

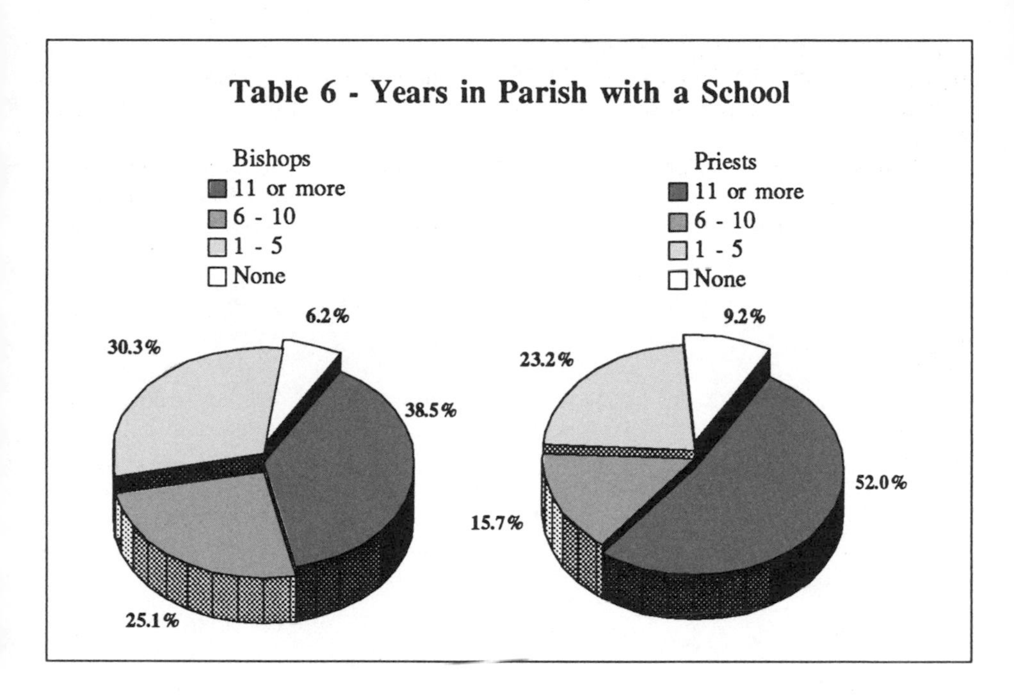
Table 6 - Years in Parish with a School
Bishops
11 or more
6 - 10
1 - 5
None
Priests
11 or more
6 - 10
1 - 5
None
6.2%
30.3%
38.5%
25.1%
9.2%
23.2%
52.0%
15.7%

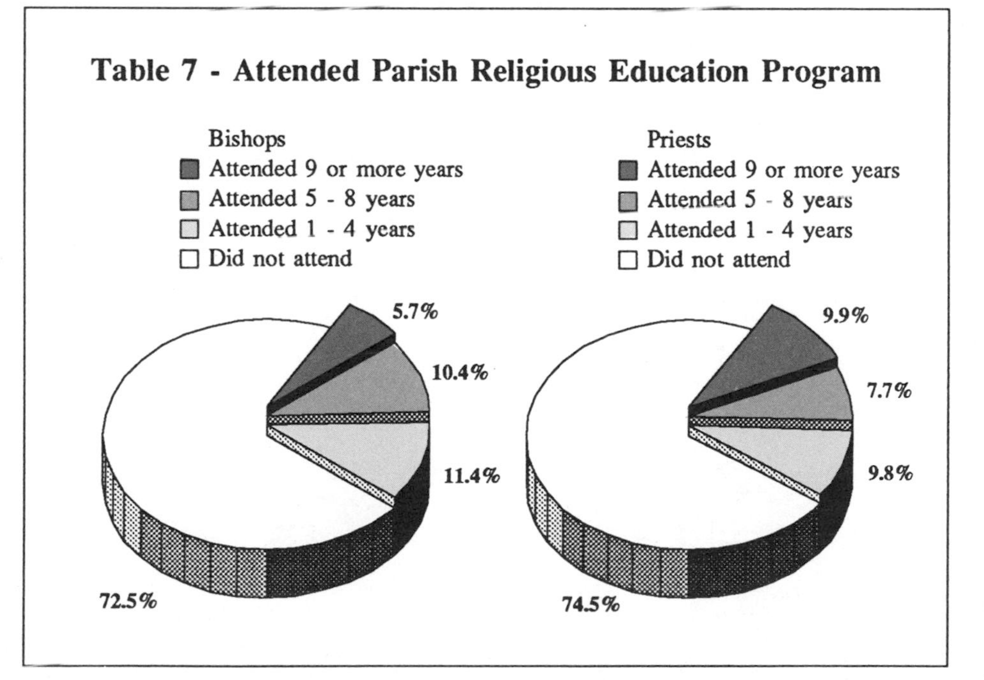
Table 7 - Attended Parish Religious Education Program
Bishops
Attended 9 or more years
Attended 5 - 8 years
Attended 1 - 4 years
Did not attend
Priests
Attended 9 or more years
Attended 5 - 8 years
Attended 1 - 4 years
Did not attend
5.7%
10.4%
11.4%
72.5%
9.9%
7.7%
9.8%
74.5%

compared to 43 percent parish implementation by the priests. The largest number of parishes who have implemented the RCIA is found in the Southeastern section of the country (85%), followed by the Great Lakes (71%), the West (63%), and the Plains (54%).

There seems to be a relationship between the age of priests and the implementation of the RCIA, with the younger clergy leading the way. Urban (73%) and suburban parishes (70%) have done more work in this area than inner-city (49%) or rural parishes (44%) (Table C7, Appendix C).

Summary

The profile of the United States bishops and priests is not different from the one previously reported in *Mixed Messages*. The new information is that over half of the bishops and even more of the priests have been moderators of parish religious education programs. And one quarter of them have been participants in parish religious education programs for at least part of their formative years. An additional piece of new information is that the RCIA has not been implemented very widely in half of the country.

CHAPTER 2:

THE PURPOSE AND VALUE OF PARISH RELIGIOUS EDUCATION PROGRAMS

The General Purposes of Parish Programs

Almost every Roman Catholic parish in the United States has some form of religious education program. Since bishops and priests have the ultimate responsibility for the operation of these programs, they were questioned concerning their perceptions of the overall purposes and values these programs have for the church.

Fundamental Purposes

Bishops and priests were in agreement regarding some of the fundamental purposes of parish religious education programs. They were almost unanimous in stating that they help people grow in faith into mature adult Christians, that they assist parents in their role as those primarily and principally responsible for the education of their children, and that they should help participants understand and articulate why they are Catholic (Table 8).

There is little doubt, therefore, about the importance bishops and priests place on religious education. As one bishop among many commented, "Religious education is of the greatest importance to the church now and in the future." A typical priest's comment was: "Religious education is one of the most urgent tasks in our church in this country, especially for youth."

Although there was slightly less than unanimous agreement that parish religious education programs should help people become active Catholics (measured by regular Mass attendance and reception of the sacraments), almost 90 percent of the bishops and 87 percent of the priests said they should. There was some variation among the priests according to the number of years they had been ordained (Table C8, Appendix C).

Purpose and Content

There was near unanimity regarding the statement that programs should help participants understand and articulate why they are Catholic. However, when the question was framed in terms of doctrine, there was less agreement. Only 76 percent of the bishops and 68 percent of the priests agreed that the main purpose of religious

Table 8 - The General Purposes of Parish Programs		
	Respondents	
Questions	Bishops Agreed %	Priests Agreed %
Main purpose is to help people grow in faith into adult Christians (21)[1]	99.0	99.0
Purpose is to assist parents in their role (17)	97.0	97.1
Purpose is to help people become active Catholics, measured by Sunday Mass and sacraments (25)	89.6	86.8
Main purpose is to communicate sound doctrine to children and youth (40)	75.9	68.4
Should help participants understand and articulate why they are Catholic (29)	98.5	97.1
Besides doctrine, programs should lead to prayer, service, and experience of community (36)	99.5	98.7
Real purpose for programs for children and youth is effect on adults (catechists and parents) (45)	14.8	23.6

[1]The number in parenthesis indicates the question number in the original questionnaire found in Appendix B.

education is to communicate sound doctrine to children and youth.

In their comments, some priests framed the question in terms of doctrinal illiteracy. One priest wrote: "There is an incredible illiteracy among young Catholic adults, even those entering the seminary. They are vaguely Christian and unaware of the richness of our Catholic heritage." Another commented: "In the past decades religious education has improved in so many ways! Yet it seems that our youth are getting more illiterate as Catholics." Still another priest bluntly stated that "When the Church abandoned the teaching of doctrine 25 years ago, we are now reaping the harvest. Most Catholic parents of young children are doctrinally illiterate."

Kelly, Benson, and Donahue (1986) concluded that a major problem with even the best catechetical programs for children and youth was the question of what they called the "cognitive content." They found that "emphasis on the doctrine and content of the faith declines over time . . . ." As the students grow older, there is less emphasis on content and more on other issues, such as interpersonal relations. They concluded that as important as these things are, an understanding of faith must mature at the same rate as other knowledge (pp. 37, 48).

Priests differed about the centrality of communicating sound doctrine according to regions of the country, with the lowest agreement coming from the West where only 56 percent of the priests agreed. Pastors and associates had the same percentage of agreement (71%) that the communication of doctrine was essential, whereas team ministry (31%) and non-parish (65%) were in less agreement. Those priests who had full-time experience in teaching or administration in a Catholic school agreed more (75%) than those who had not (63%). Those priests who have implemented the RCIA were agreed less (62%) than those who had not (79%) (Table C9, Appendix C). However, bishops and priests were almost unanimous in affirming the four-fold purpose of religious education, namely, doctrine, worship, service, and community (Table 8).

Catechists and Parents

Bishops and priests generally did not agree that the purpose for the church's having religious education programs for children and youth is for the effects that it has on adult catechists and parents. Only 15 percent of the bishops and 24 percent of the priests agreed (Table 8). Those bishops who had been moderators of parish religious education programs were slightly more inclined (20%) to say that all programs focus on adults, compared to those who were not (9%).

Surprisingly, those priests who had been ordained the longest agreed at twice the rate of the other priests that the main purpose of programs for children and youth was for adults. Also more pastors (27%) than associates (17%) thought that religious education programs were aimed primarily at adults than did other priests (Table C10, Appendix C).

The Value of Parish Programs

With near unanimity, bishops and priests agreed that parish religious education programs perform an essential service for the church. They also agreed that parish programs should encompass a whole range of activities that engage people throughout life, and that programs should teach people to think critically about religion and society (Table 9). Those bishops who had been moderators of religious education programs agreed almost unanimously about the range of activities at 97 percent compared to 89 percent for those who had not (Table C11, Appendix C).

Years of ordination differentiated the perceptions of some bishops in regard to critical thinking. Compared to the near unanimity of the other age groups, only 89 percent of the bishops aged 56 to 65 thought that critical thinking was an integral part of religious education (Table C12, Appendix C).

Table 9 - The Value of Parish Programs

	Respondents	
Questions	Bishops Agreed %	Priests Agreed %
Elementary and secondary programs (CCD) perform an essential service for the church (13)	99.5	98.4
Should encompass a range of programs throughout life, beginning with early childhood (35)	93.3	94.5
Should teach people to think critically about religion and society (14)	94.4	90.5

The Content of Parish Programs

The content of catechesis is a particular concern of the contemporary church. Two issues seem of special importance and both are covered in the NCD. The first is authority and its relationship to church teaching. As the NCD states:

> Thus, the bishop holds the primary position of authority over programs of catechesis. Under him the pastor holds the office of direct responsibility in the local Church. The teaching of what is opposed to the faith of the Catholic Church, its doctrinal and moral positions, its laws, discipline, and practice should in no way be allowed or countenanced in catechetical programs on any level (1979, #47).

In the same paragraph, the NCD touches the second issue, that of presenting the entire Christian message: "Since catechesis seeks to foster mature faith in individuals and communities, it is careful to present the Christian message in its entirety (1979, #47).

As reported earlier, bishops and priests overwhelmingly agreed that parish religious education programs should help participants understand and articulate why they are Catholic (Table 8). They also agreed that religious literacy should be a major goal of every program (96% for bishops and 90% for priests). Further, 91 percent of the bishops and 88 percent of the priests agreed that the programs should help participants attain a working knowledge of religious terms (Table 10). Those priests involved in team ministry and non-parish work agreed almost unanimously that a knowledge of religious terms is important as a measure of success for parish programs, compared to 87 percent of pastors and 84 percent of associates (Table C13, Appendix C).

However, when bishops and priests were asked if the most important part of any religious education program is instruction in the doctrines of the faith, the percentages of agreement dropped substantially, as they had in the previous question about doctrine. Only 79 percent of the bishops and 68 percent of the priests agreed with that statement(Table 10). Agreement about instruction in doctrine seems to be a function

Table 10 - Content of Religious Education

	Respondents	
Questions	Bishops Agreed %	Priests Agreed %
Religious literacy should be a major goal of every program (55)	95.9	89.7
To be successful, should help participants attain a working knowledge of religious terms (32)	91.4	88.0
Most important part of program is instruction in the doctrines of faith (26)	78.7	67.9
Universal catechism from Holy See will be a great help in improving programs (18)	81.6	63.1
Programs should always include scripture study (49)	100.00	97.2

of age, with the older clergy tending to agree more than the younger. Role also has some influence; only 20 percent of the priests in team ministry agreed concerning doctrine. There are also regional differences with priests in the Mideast (59%) and the West (56%) showing the lowest agreement (Table C14, Appendix C).

Those priests who were in a parish that has implemented the RCIA had a lower perception that doctrine was the most important part of religious education programs; 62 percent of those priests agreed compared to 74 percent of those who do not have the RCIA. Over 62 percent of the priests who had attended a parish religious education program agreed with the statement about doctrine, compared to 81 percent of those who had never attended (Table C14, Appendix C).

Although it is not possible to state with certitude why this particular question received less agreement than the ones on religious literacy, it might be that "instruction in the doctrines of the faith" sounds more ideological than the wording of the other two questions. It is also possible that the term "most important" caused people to answer the question differently.

Nevertheless, large percentages of bishops and priests see doctrine as an important question in religious education. Several bishops wrote reflections similar to these: "Following Jesus Christ and His Church and the Magisterium must be emphasized in religious education programs to be truly effective and in accord with Vatican II documents." Several priests also commented along the same lines: "Above all, religious education must be based on the authentic teaching of the Church, in full accord with the Magisterium."

Table 10 also shows that four out of five bishops, but only three out of five priests, thought that the universal catechism will be a great help in improving parish programs. Once again, age seemed to make a difference in the responses; in general, the older the priest, the more inclined he was to see the universal catechism as helpful. Those priests whose parishes have implemented the RCIA were less inclined (60%) to see the universal catechism as helpful than those whose parishes have not (72%) (Table C15, Appendix C).

There was no question in any bishop's mind that parish religious education programs should always include scripture study; 97 percent of the priests agreed (Table 10).

Faith and Life

There was overwhelming agreement among the bishops and priests that there should be a close relationship between what a person believes and what that person experiences in daily living. Two priests' comments were typical: "Too often we are content with mere instruction of our young people and adults without having programs that help to arrive at a faith experience" and "Catholic religious instruction, in its present state, leaves the young person with little or no sense of Roman Catholic identity nor of the connection between their lives and the challenge of living the gospel in the world."

There is some indication that the connection is critical. Programs that emphasize content plus life-skills and tie the two together have greater success. Programs that have been judged successful "find creative ways for students to learn that faith speaks to life and the many decisions and choices it presents" and help the students make "faith relevant to the turmoil of adolescence" (Kelly, et al., 1986, p. 50).

The bishops and priests thought that religious education should emphasize the relationship between faith and life experiences, that it should encompass a whole range of programs and activities that engage Catholics throughout life, that the programs should include activities for people of every age, and that, to be authentically Catholic, religious education must include social justice as a major dimension (Table 11). On the last item, those priests who have implemented the RCIA agreed more strongly (95% to 86%) than those who have not.

Table 11 - Faith and Life

	Respondents	
Questions	Bishops Agreed %	Priests Agreed %
Programs should emphasize relationship between faith and life experiences (22)	98.5	98.1
Programs should include activities for people in every age and stage of life (38)	97.4	95.8
To be authentically Catholic, program must include social justice as a major dimension (43)	93.4	90.5
Programs for children and youth should require participation in social service programs (52)	83.9	76.2

In regard to programs requiring children and youth to participate in social service programs, bishops and priests agreed less strongly. Almost 84 percent of the bishops and 76 percent of the priests thought that there should be some participation. Bishops were divided along regional lines. Only 67 percent of New England and 70 percent of the Mideast bishops agreed. The bishops in the rest of the country were more favorable toward that kind of student participation. Also, those bishops who had worked full-time in a Catholic school agreed at a rate of 91 percent compared to 78 percent for those who had not (Table C16, Appendix C).

More priests who have implemented the RCIA (81%) thought programs should include social service activity than did those who have not (68%). However, priests who have had experience as moderators of parish religious education programs only agreed at 72 percent, compared to 83 percent for those who were never moderators. Perhaps their experiences have shown them the difficulty in organizing such activities (Table C16, Appendix C).

Summary

Bishops and priests have basically the same vision of the purpose and value of parish programs. These programs should help people grow in faith into mature Christians, should be authentically Catholic, should help people see faith as an integral part of life, and should help parents in their role as educators.

They were also nearly unanimous in saying that parish programs should cover a range of activities that start in early childhood and go throughout life and that they should teach people to think critically about religion and society.

The bishops and priests moved more toward unanimity when the statements were phrased in terms of action than they did when they were more static in their formulation. For example, to say that religious education helps people understand and articulate their faith received nearly unanimous agreement. To say that its purpose is to communicate doctrine received less concurrence.

More bishops than priests saw the universal catechism as a great help in improving parish programs; but the older the priest, the more inclined he was to see it as helpful. Both bishops and priests agreed that any religious education program should include scripture study.

Bishops and priests were almost unanimous in their thinking that programs should emphasize the relationship between faith and daily living, should lead to an understanding of doctrine, prayer, service and an experience of community, and should include activities for people in every age and stage of life.

Although they agreed very strongly that, to be authentically Catholic, programs must include social justice as a major dimension, they were not as strong in saying that the programs should require participation in a social service program.

CHAPTER 3:

THE EFFECTIVENESS OF PARISH RELIGIOUS EDUCATION PROGRAMS

Children and Youth

Andrew Greeley (1985) has written that there is no evidence that parish religious education programs are effective (pp. 133-139). The majority of bishops and priests did not agree. Over 84 percent of the bishops and 78 percent of the priests thought that elementary and secondary parish religious education programs have measurable, positive effects on adult religious behavior (Table 12).

However, not everyone agreed that effectiveness in religious education programs can be measured. A bishop wrote that "Presently, we have no valid way of measuring the effectiveness of our current evangelization processes with children and youth. This makes it very difficult to answer questions about effectiveness."

Table 12 - Adults, Youth, and Children

Questions	Respondents Bishops Agreed %	Respondents Priests Agreed %
Elementary and secondary programs have measurable, positive effects on adult behavior (44)	84.1	77.9
Elementary programs are more effective than secondary (58)	75.0	62.9
Secondary programs are just as effective as elementary (60)	22.7	33.6
Parish renewal programs (like RENEW) are effective adult catechetical programs and should be encouraged (56)	92.6	81.2
Program effectiveness for children and youth is in direct proportion to adult program effectiveness (62)	39.0	42.4

Bishops who thought their dioceses have implemented the RCIA agreed that programs have measurable effects even more strongly than other bishops, 87 to 74 percent. The older the priests, the more likely they were to agree that programs have measurable effects; for example, 84 percent of the priests 66 and over agreed, while only 59 percent of those 35 and under did. Somewhat surprisingly, only 74 percent of those who had been moderators of parish religious education programs agreed, compared to 85 percent for those who had not (Table C17, Appendix C).

Elementary and Secondary

In terms of the long-running question about which program is more effective, 75 percent of the bishops and 63 percent of the priests agreed that elementary programs are more effective than secondary. Among the bishops, there were some differences based on age (Table C18, Appendix C).

For the priests, the youngest were less convinced (44%) that elementary programs were more effective than secondary, compared to much higher rates among the older clergy. Among the regions of the country, New England (41%) and the West (54%) were less sure that one group was more effective than another.

There were also differences among priests based on the number of years spent in a parish with a school. Those who had never been in a parish with a school only agreed that elementary was more effective at 30 percent. Those who had never attended a Catholic secondary school also agreed at the relatively low rate of 49 percent. More secular priests (66%) than religious priests (52%) saw elementary programs more effective than secondary (Table C19, Appendix C).

Only 23 percent of the bishops and 34 percent of the priests thought that secondary programs were as effective as elementary (Table 12). Those bishops who had worked full-time in a Catholic school had an agreement rate of 26 percent, as compared to 47 percent for those who had never worked in a school. Participation in Catholic secondary education made a difference among the priests, 31 percent to 41 percent; and years in a parish with a school also seemed to have an effect. Priests who had never worked in a school agreed that secondary programs are as effective as elementary at 65 percent compared to slightly over 30 percent for those who had (Table C20, Appendix C).

Adult Education

As Table 12 indicates, bishops and priests saw parish renewal programs such as RENEW as effective adult catechetical programs and thought they should be encouraged. Although two bishops pointed out that RENEW specifically states that it is not a catechetical program, in many parishes the people involved in religious education participate, encourage and administer the program for the parish. Many religious educators would agree that it does have catechetical implications.

Enthusiasm for renewal programs seems to be in inverse proportion to the number of years priests have been ordained. The most enthusiasm came from those ordained ten years and under (91%) and the least from those ordained 41 years and over (63%). Also, 85 percent of those priests who have implemented the RCIA thought parish renewal programs should be encouraged, compared to 75 percent of those who have not (Table C21, Appendix C).

Bishops and priests did not see much of a relationship between the effectiveness of programs for children and youth and the effectiveness of parish programs for adults. Only 39 percent of the bishops and 42 percent of the priests thought the effectiveness of these programs was directly related to one another (Table 12). Those bishops whose dioceses have implemented the RCIA were more inclined to see the relationship (45%) than those whose dioceses have not (21%) (Table C22, Appendix C).

Only 39 percent of those priests who have been in a parish with a school thought that program effectiveness for children and youth is in direct proportion to the effectiveness of adult programs, compared to 78 percent who had not. The longer a priest had spent in a parish with a school, the less inclined he was to see a relationship between adult education and education for children and youth. Only 37 percent of the secular priests saw the relationship, compared to 59 percent of religious (Table C22, Appendix C).

Ingredients for Effective Programs

Bishops and priests were in general agreement on the ingredients for effective religious education programs. They thought that programs that have clear written goals, have the active support and involvement of parents, have a pastor who is visibly supportive, and have regular ways for parishioners to evaluate and improve them are more effective than those that do not (Table 13).

Priests who are assigned to the inner city and to rural parishes were less certain that regular ways for parishioners to evaluate programs are as important as do priests in the urban and suburban areas. Those priests who have not implemented the RCIA also did not see regular evaluation as related to effectiveness as strongly as those who had (Table C23, Appendix C).

Table 13 - Ingredients for Effective Programs

Questions	Respondents Bishops Agreed %	Respondents Priests Agreed %
Programs with clear, written goals are more effective than those without (19)	97.0	94.5
Parents' support and involvement are critical for programs for children (53)	99.5	98.1
The pastor must be visibly supportive for successful parish programs (31)	99.0	94.4
Programs that have regular ways for parishioners to evaluate them are more effective (27)	91.4	85.9
The most effective programs have a fulltime professional director of religious education (DRE) (16)	80.7	78.0
The more funding, the more effective the program (15)	69.1	61.7

Director of Religious Education

The most effective religious education programs have a paid, full-time professional director of religious education (DRE) according to 81 percent of the bishops and 78 percent of the priests (Table 13). Those bishops who had been full-time in a Catholic school agreed at the higher rate of 89 percent compared to 75 percent of those who had not (Table C24, Appendix C).

Priests' perceptions varied according to their role, their assignment, their attendance at religious education, and their years in a parish with a school. Pastors were less inclined to see the presence of a professional DRE as connected to effectiveness than were associates. Although 72 percent of the pastors thought that a professional DRE is essential, 89 percent of the associates did. Priests in the inner city and rural areas saw the professional DRE as much less important than priests in urban and suburban areas. Part of that difference may be connected to finances, since inner city and rural parishes would be less likely to have the funds necessary to pay a professional.

The more years a priest attended a parish religious education program, the less likely he was to see a DRE as necessary. Only 58 percent of those who attended religious education programs nine years or more saw a DRE as essential, compared to 80 percent of those who had never attended religious education. Although there were few if any professional parish religious educators when most priests participated, that fact alone does not explain the perceptions. If there had been differences based on the ages of the priests, those differences would have explained to some degree why priests who attended a parish program would be less likely to find the DRE necessary. Since there was none, the reasons for the differences cannot be explained.

Years in a parish with a school also made a difference; 89 percent of the priests who had never been in a parish with a school thought that a DRE was essential, compared to 75 percent for those who had spent eleven or more years in a parish with a school (Table C25, Appendix C).

Those priests who have implemented the RCIA saw a DRE as important at a rate of 84 percent compared to 68 percent for those who have not implemented the RCIA. Surprisingly, only 73 percent of those priests who had been a moderator of a parish program agreed that a DRE is important, compared to 86 percent of those who had never been a moderator (Table C25, Appendix C).

Funding

The final ingredient for an effective program is funding. Only 69 percent of the bishops and 62 percent of the priests thought that in general the more funding available to religious education programs, the more effective they will be (Table 13). These percentages reflect some caution about tying money too directly to effectiveness. A previous study concluded that quality does not result primarily from the amount of money spent. Adequate funding is certainly necessary for effectiveness, but money without planning and leadership will not accomplish the goal (Kelly, et al., 1986, pp. 47-48).

The bishops ordained 31 to 40 years, that is, ages 56 through 65, were even less convinced (58%) that funding would make a major difference. The priests in the

Mideast region had a significantly higher percentage of agreement than did the rest of the country; 79 percent of those priests thought that the more funding, the more effective the program (Table C26, Appendix C).

Structures and Effectiveness

For any institution, structures are important. The way the institution usually impacts people individually is through its structures. Therefore, the kinds of structures that parish religious education programs have are important to the students and the church in general.

The Common Model

Bishops and priests were not convinced of the effectiveness of the most common parish religious education structure. When asked if the current structure, that is, a one to one-and-one-half hour class for approximately thirty weeks a year, is effective, only 38 percent of the bishops and 41 percent of the priests responded affirmatively (Table 14). There were, however, major differences in how the priests responded based on their number of years ordained, their role, and the number of years in a parish with a school.

Table 14 - Structures and Effectiveness

Questions	Respondents: Bishops Agreed %	Respondents: Priests Agreed %
Current structure for parish programs (one to one and one-half hours for 30 weeks) is effective (23)	37.7	41.0
The current "classroom" or "school" model should be changed (33)	25.5	45.6
The programs in my diocese (bishops) or parish (priests) are generally effective (30)	78.5	77.1
Although they could be improved, parish programs are generally effective (64)	73.0	72.2

The longer a priest had been ordained, the more likely he was to respond that the current structure is effective. For example, 56 percent of the priests ordained 40 years and over said that the current structure is effective, compared to only 18 percent of those ordained ten years and under. Pastors were much more likely to say the programs were effective (47%) than were associates (29%); and 58 percent of those priests who had never been in a parish with a school thought that the current structure was effective, compared to 47 percent of those who had been for eleven years or more (Table C27, Appendix C).

Progress and Change

Even though a large majority of the bishops and priests thought that the current model of religious education is ineffective, when asked if the "classroom" model should be changed, only 26 percent of the bishops and 46 percent of the priests agreed. The older priests agreed even less than the younger ones. Those ordained 31 to 40 years and those ordained 41 years and over agreed at 36 percent and 25 percent respectively. Those who had been full-time in a Catholic school agreed at a lower rate (37% to 52%) than those who had never been full-time (Table C28, Appendix C).

At first glance it might be somewhat mystifying why the bishops and priests would say that a model was ineffective and yet be unwilling to change it. Their responses to a question about effectiveness close to home may provide the answer. When asked if the religious education programs "in my diocese" (for bishops) and "in my parish" (for priests) are generally effective, 79 percent of the bishops and 77 percent of the priests said that they were.

For bishops, the longer they had been pastors, the more convinced they were that their local programs are effective. For priests, pastors agreed that the programs are effective at 84 percent compared to 73 percent for associates. Those who had implemented the RCIA were 82 percent, compared to 72 percent to those who had not; and 80 percent of the diocesan priests, as contrasted to 68 percent of the religious community priests, thought that programs in their parishes were generally effective (Table C29, Appendix C).

Thus it is possible to interpret the responses as saying that the typical model, the "classroom" model, is ineffective every place but in "my diocese" or "my parish."

In response to a parallel question, 73 percent of the bishops and 72 percent of the priests said that although parish religious education programs could be improved, they are generally effective (Table 14). Pastors were consistent in being more convinced (78%) than associates (65%). There were also significant differences based on how long a priest had been in a parish with a school. Those who had never been in a parish with a school tended to agree with those who had been in a school for eleven years or more (approximately 80%) compared to those who had been in a parish with a school for one to ten years (approximately 63%) (Table C30, Appendix C). Several priests observed that the general improvement sought would come through better "teacher training" and "coordination of efforts" among all parish educators.

Strong Feelings

Bishops and priests obviously did not take the question of effectiveness lightly. And if the number of written comments is any indication of strong feelings, this area was one about which bishops and priests have deep convictions. Although a majority was favorable about the effectiveness of religious education, the comments were almost exclusively negative.

Bishops' comments were milder than those of the priests. "I have a strong suspicion that generally Religious Education Programs in the country are not effective." According to another bishop, the reason for this opinion is that "They do not have the time with the young women and men in order to do the job properly." One bishop lamented that "Protestant Bible Schools seem to bring about 'conversion' more effectively than Catholic methods. Kids see religion as just another class among Catholics. Protestants center on belief in Jesus as a living force throughout life."

Priests were less circumspect than most of the bishops. "I have yet to see a CCD program at any level that was effective." The main problem, according to a pastor, is "getting the people to attend classes, instruction, or whatever. But as Yogi Berra once said, 'If people don't want to go to ball games, you can't stop them!'" Another pastor wrote that the problem is the loss of women religious. "When we had the sisters staffing our CCD programs it seems there was more in depth teaching of Catholic doctrine. The laity are not really fully trained so our Catholic instruction generally suffers."

A pastor and diocesan vicar wrote that professional educators are not the answer either. "'Professional' people and 'programs' are not going to do it for religious ed. Holy teachers steeped in the traditions and truths of our Church and who are able to articulate their faith in a contemporary manner will be effective. 'Social dimensions', 'experience of community', 'family centered programs' only deflect from the poverty of substance with which our 'modern' approaches to truth are replete."

One bishop's comments did reflect the majority thinking: "Programs are much better than 5 - 10 years ago. I am grateful for the excellent programs in the diocese. I am hoping for continued emphasis on content and the knowledge , understanding, and application (experience) in living out the faith in our daily lives."

Catholic Schools

In 1986 bishops and priests were surveyed on their perceptions of the role of Catholic schools within the church. The results were published in *Mixed Messages* and parallel the responses to the three questions about Catholic schools in the present survey.

Cost Effectiveness

Table 15 shows that the majority of bishops and priests did not think that parish religious education programs for children and youth are more cost-effective than Catholic schools. Although only 32 percent of the bishops and 47 percent of the priests thought that parish programs are a more effective use of the church's money, slightly over half of the clergy ordained thirty years and under (55 years old and younger) thought that parish programs are more cost effective (Table C31, Appendix C).

As might be expected, priests in the Mideast (34%) and the Great Lakes (42%) had a low agreement rate with equality of cost-effectiveness. By far the largest majority of Catholic school students are in those two regions. The West (65%) and the Southwest (59%) have the largest percentages of priests who thought that religious education programs are more cost-effective than schools.

Whether a priest had attended a Catholic elementary school also made a difference. The less time a priest spent in Catholic elementary school, the more he tended to view parish programs as more cost-effective than schools (Table C31, Appendix C).

Program Effectiveness

A large majority of the bishops (92%) and a lesser majority of the priests (70%)

Table 15 - Catholic Schools

Questions	Respondents Bishops Agreed %	Priests Agreed %
Parish programs for children and youth are more cost effective than Catholic schools (41)	31.6	46.6
Catholic schools are the best means available to the church for the religious education of children and youth (37)	91.8	70.1
Catholic schools should be supported and new ones built (59)	82.8	56.5

thought that Catholic schools are the best means for religious education of children and youth in the church (Table 15). This statement parallels a similar finding from the earlier survey (O'Brien, 1987b, pp. 73-74).

As was also the case in the past, those priests who were ordained eleven to twenty years (ages 38 to 47) had a significantly lower level of agreement. Only a small majority of that age group (55%) thought that Catholic schools are the best means of church education. Role also made a difference. Pastors (74%) were more favorable toward the effectiveness of Catholic schools than associates (69%).

There were also regional differences among the priests. Those from the Plains (87%), the Great Lakes (78%), and the Mideast (78%) were far more likely to see Catholic schools as the best church education than were priests from the West (47%), New England (56%), or the Southeast (66%) (Table C32, Appendix C).

Also, those priests who had been in parishes with a school were more favorable than those who had not, as were those who had been involved full-time in a Catholic school. However, those who had not implemented the RCIA were more favorable toward schools than those who had (Table C32, Appendix C).

When questioned about whether, given the church's commitment to religious education, Catholic schools should be supported and new ones built, 83 percent of the bishops and 57 percent of the priests agreed that they should be (Table 15). This finding also parallels the results from *Mixed Messages*, where 88 percent of the bishops and 61 percent of the priests thought that new schools should be built (O'Brien, 1987b, p. 92).

Opinions on Schools

Most of the bishops who commented on schools were positive. Several wrote of the need for cooperation between schools "and religious education programs since they are both part of an educational effort involving the entire parish." Others praised the schools. "Catholic schools are still the best form of religious education. Ideally the training of parents for the formation and education of children would be ideal, but it doesn't work out practically in the great majority of cases."

Another bishop wrote: "My support of Catholic schools does not flow from the hope that we can reach all Catholic children and young people in this way. We cannot. But Catholic schools, requiring extraordinary sacrifice, make a dramatic statement of how important the Church considers education to be. The parish must make equal sacrifices for effective education for public school Catholic students. How is the question."

Unlike the bishops, the majority of the comments from the priests were negative. They centered almost exclusively on costs: "Proportionally, too much money is spent on Catholic schools and too little on R.E. R.E. is still the step-child." A pastor wrote: "The cost of Catholic schools is becoming so great that other needed programs, including CCD, are suffering disastrously. Many parishes and dioceses have priced the poor out of Catholic schools." In the same vein, another priest said: "When a parish is called to supplement the school resources out of its collection and as a result no longer can afford a trained DRE or allow for the funds for a comprehensive religious ed program for all in the parish, we need to look at and reflect on what we are doing."

Summary

Bishops and priests thought that parish programs have measurable positive effects on adult religious behavior. However, they did not see much of a direct relationship between effective adult programs and those for children and youth. They viewed elementary programs as clearly more effective than secondary. For adults, they thought parish renewal programs effective enough to warrant encouragement.

The criteria for effective programs, in their view, included written goals, an evaluation, parental involvement, and the support of the pastor. Over three quarters thought that the most effective programs have a full-time, professional DRE, although there was an inverse proportion between the number of years a priest had been a participant in a parish program and his perception of the need for a DRE. Slightly more than half saw increases in funding connected to increases in effectiveness.

The classroom model, the most common model of religious education, was judged ineffective by approximately six out of ten of the bishops and priests. Associates were less likely to think the model effective than were pastors. However, neither bishops nor priests wanted to change the model, possibly because they viewed their own programs as effective.

Catholic schools were still seen as the best means of religious education and as not less cost effective than parish religious education programs. A high percentage of the nation's bishops but only half of the priests thought Catholic schools should be supported and new ones built.

CHAPTER 4:

ADMINISTRATION AND STRUCTURE OF PARISH RELIGIOUS EDUCATION PROGRAMS

Responsibilities

With any kind of program, someone has to have the responsibility for quality control. The bishops were almost unanimous (97%) and the priests only slightly less so (86%) that the diocese has a responsibility to ensure quality religious education programs in each parish. They were equally in agreement that a parish program operates best with strong support services from the diocese (98% for bishops and 90% for priests) (Table 16).

Bishops and priests were divided, however, on whether or not the diocese should establish uniform religious education programs in each parish. Only 57 percent of the bishops and 41 percent of the priests agreed (Table 16). There was a sharp division among the different age groups. The older the priest, the more likely he was to want the diocese to establish consistency in religious education. Although 60 percent of the older priests thought that the diocese should establish uniform programs, only 34 percent of those 35 and under would agree (Table C33, Appendix C).

Bishops (98%) and priests (88%) were very clear that the pastor has the overall responsibility for the parish program (Table 16). However, the inner city and suburban priests agreed at a higher rate than the urban and rural. The reasons for those differences are not clear (Table C34, Appendix C).

There was near unanimity among the bishops and priests (99% and 98%) that catechist training is an important responsibility of the pastor and the professional religious educator. Bishops and pastors saw priests as an integral part of the parish program.

There was less unanimity, although still a strong perception (92% for bishops and 82% for priests) that every parish religious education program needs a board or committee (Table 16). There were some regional differences. Bishops and priests from the Southeast, Plains, Great Lakes and West were significantly more interested in having a board or committee for religious education than were those of New England or the

Table 16 - Responsibilities		
	Respondents	
	Bishops	Priests
	Agreed	Agreed
Questions	%	%
The (arch)diocese has the responsibility to ensure quality programs in each parish (39)	97.0	86.0
A parish program operates best with with strong support services from the (arch)diocese (24)	97.5	90.4
The (arch)diocese should establish uniform programs in each parish (48)	56.6	41.0
Pastor has overall responsibility for the program (34)	97.5	87.9
Catechist training is an important responsibility of the pastor and DRE (28)	99.0	97.7
A board or committee is an important part of a parish program (20)	91.9	82.0

Mideast. Not surprisingly, those priests who implemented the RCIA were more favorable than those who had not, probably because they work more often with groups (Table C35, Appendix C).

Adult Education

Quoting the *General Catechetical Directory* from the Holy See, the NCD states that "While aiming to enrich the faith life of individuals at their particular stages of development, every form of catechesis is oriented in some way to the catechesis of adults, who are capable of a full response to God's word (1979, #32)." The NCD also notes that the emphasis on adult catechesis must not take away from the church's catechetical commitment to children (1979, #40).

Adults and Youth

Bishops and priests concurred. They did not think that the church should concentrate its efforts on adult religious education rather than on children and youth. Only 13 percent of the bishops and 29 percent of the priests thought that adults should be the exclusive group receiving religious education (Table 17). As one priest put it, "I don't believe we have to make a choice between adult or child education. It must be both."

In general, the older the priest, the less likely he was to say that the church should concentrate on adults. The one exception was the 36 to 45 year age group. They would tend to agree with priests 56 and older. Pastors were less inclined to concentrate the church's efforts on adult education than associates (28% to 33%), as were those who have been full-time in a Catholic school, 23% compared to 35% for those who had not (Table C36, Appendix C).

Since the RCIA does deal with adults, it would be expected that a higher percentage

Table 17 - Adult Education		
	Respondents	
Questions	Bishops Agreed %	Priests Agreed %
Church should concentrate its efforts on adult religious education, rather than on children and youth (51)	13.1	29.2
The RCIA is the best hope for having knowledgeable and faith-filled Catholics in the future (57)	78.7	59.1
Sacramental preparation programs for for parents are the most common form of adult education (46)	81.0	79.8

of priests who had implemented the RCIA would opt for concentration on adult religious education. That is the case, 35 percent to 22 percent (Table C36, Appendix C).

Hope for the Future

Priests and bishops were divided on their perceptions of the RCIA as the best hope for having knowledgeable and faith-filled Catholics in the future. Because it involves so many people in the parish, it seems that it would affect a large number of adults. Although 79 percent of the bishops thought that the RCIA is a hope for the future, only 59 percent of the priests agreed with them (Table 17).

The bishops had some regional differences, with the bishops in the Plains, New England and the Mideast being the least enthusiastic about the RCIA as a great hope for the future (Table C37, Appendix C). This perception is consistent with their previously reported perceptions of whether or not their dioceses have implemented the RCIA (Table C7, Appendix C).

Those priests who have implemented the RCIA placed more hope in it than those who have not (67% to 47%). There were also differences among priests according to how many years they had been in a parish with a school; those priests who had been in such a parish for 11 or more years were significantly less likely to see the RCIA as a great hope for the future than those with less or no experience in a parish with a school.

The same thing was true of those who had been full-time at a Catholic school. They were less enthusiastic about the RCIA (52%) than those who had never been full-time (65%). Those priests who had been moderators of parish religious education programs agreed; only 54 percent of those saw the RCIA as a hope, compared to 66 percent of those who had never been a moderator (Table C37, Appendix C).

Sacramental Preparation

Because of the importance of adult education, bishops and priests were asked if in most parishes the sacramental preparation programs for parents were the most common form. In response, 81 percent of the bishops and 80 percent of the priests agreed that, in fact, sacramental preparation programs are the most common form of adult education

(Table 17).

Those priests who had been ordained the least amount of time tended to see sacramental preparation as the most prevalent form of adult education, with the youngest group almost unanimous. Because associates were generally younger than pastors, it follows that associates (86%) also saw sacramental preparation as the most common form of adult education more often than did pastors (74%) (Table C38, Appendix C).

Unfortunately the best evidence is that in spite of the importance church documents give to adult education it has not received a high priority in practice. According to a report by Mahoney (1987) to the Department of Education of the United States Catholic Conference (USCC) entitled *Effective and Faithful: Catechetical Ministry in the United States, A Study of the Studies*, sacramental preparation is the major form of adult education found in most parishes. "While slightly over half of the parishes did have some type of program for adults, other than that accompanying sacramental preparation of children, this could not be seen as a high priority for the parishes" (p. 24). Quoting his own study, Mahoney also stated that parishioners do not place the same priority on adult education as they do on religious education for children and youth (Mahoney, 1987, p. 21).

Family-Centered Programs

The church has always recognized the important role of the family in religious education. In church documents, parents are called "the first and foremost catechists of their children" (NCD, 1979, #212). Thus the church recognizes the efforts of many parishes to offer family-centered religious education programs that bring families together to help them carry out their responsibilities in the church's educational mission (NCD, 1979, #226). Unfortunately there are no data concerning the number of family-centered programs in the United States. The guess is that the number is small.

Aware of the importance of families and consistent with their insistence on the role of parents, over 75 percent of the bishops and 79 percent of the priests agreed that family-centered religious education offers the best hope for the future of religious education (Table 18). There were some regional differences among the bishops; 89 percent of the bishops in the West and 88 percent in the Plains agreed, while only 58 percent of the bishops in New England did (Table C39, Appendix C).

Table 18 - Family-Centered Programs

	Respondents	
Questions	Bishops Agreed %	Priests Agreed %
Family-centered programs offer the best hope for the future (50)	75.1	78.8
All programs should move toward family-centered catechesis (42)	67.2	72.7

Those priests ordained eleven to twenty years were less favorable toward family-centered programs than other age groups. Members of religious communities were more inclined to see family-centered programs as a hope for the future than those who were not, 87 to 76 percent (Table C39, Appendix C).

In a parallel question, bishops and priests were asked if all parish religious education programs should move towards a model of family-centered catechesis. Only 67 percent of the bishops and 73 percent of the priests agreed (Table 18). Thus both groups were slightly less favorable toward family-centered catechesis when the statement indicated that it should become the predominant model for religious education. There were regional differences among the bishops and priests that parallelled the regional differences in the previous question, with New England and the Great Lakes showing the least enthusiasm (Table C40, Appendix C).

Years of ordination made a difference among the priests. The longer a man had been ordained, the more favorable he was toward family-centered catechesis. For example, those ordained 41 years and over were in favor at 92 percent, while those ordained eleven to twenty years were at 58 percent. The same thing is true in regard to pastors and associates, with pastors at 78 percent favorable and associates at 67 percent (Table C40, Appendix C). In what was somewhat of a surprise, suburban priests were much less in favor (59%) than their counterparts in the inner city (72%), urban (77%), and rural areas (78%). Also, those who had attended a Catholic secondary school were less favorable (69%) than those who had not (83%) (Table C40, Appendix C).

Although all bishops and priests were not willing to move toward family-centered programs, the role of parents received the largest number of comments. One bishop wrote: "I think a good family-centered catechetical program is the answer. In most cases neither Catholic schools or CCD programs do what is expected of them." Another said that "We also need to do a better job empowering parents to center their family life and personal lives on the person of Jesus Christ. Without that, we are bound to continue the present difficulties."

A number of priests expressed the same sentiments: "Religious education should begin in the Catholic home." "We need programs and ideas to involve the children's parents as much as possible." "Religious education is only effective when it involves the entire family. A good doctrine-oriented program will work only _if_ the parents work with the program."

One bishop demurred: "In general, parishes which have placed too much reliance on parental training have, in my experience, ended up very disappointed. It's the 'blind leading the blind.'"

Children and Youth

Youth Ministry

The NCD (1979) states that "youth catechesis is most effective within a total youth ministry." This kind of program responds to the unique needs of youth, is shared with youth, is directed in part by youth, and interprets the concerns of youth (#228). When asked if the church should concentrate its efforts on total youth ministry rather than on just religious education efforts for youth, 75 percent of the bishops and 79 percent of the priests agreed (Table 19).

Table 19 - Children and Youth

Questions	Respondents: Bishops Agreed %	Respondents: Priests Agreed %
Church should concentrate on total youth ministry rather than on just religious education for youth (54)	74.5	78.5
Every parish secondary program should include retreats (47)	95.4	90.2
Parish programs should begin at the preschool level (63)	80.9	78.9
Sacramental preparation should become unified for all children and youth including those in Catholic schools (61)	69.1	71.2
A separate children's liturgy of the word should be available at least at one eucharist every Sunday in every parish (65)	49.5	52.8

There was no indication why the approximately 25 percent of the bishops and priests did not agree. They certainly were very much in favor of every parish secondary program including a regular retreat program, 95 percent for bishops and 90 percent for priests (Table 19). Only the bishops in New England had a significantly lower response rate on the retreat question (75%) than the rest of the country. It was no surprise that those priests who had implemented the RCIA were more inclined to want a retreat program than those who had not (Table C41, Appendix C).

Early Childhood Religious Education

With all of the emphasis today on early childhood, most bishops (81%) and priests (79%) would like to see parish religious education programs begin at a preschool level (Table 19) (See NCD, 1979, #177). Bishops who had worked full-time in a Catholic school thought that parish programs should begin at preschool at a much higher rate (90%) than those who had never been full-time (75%). The same thing was true for those bishops who thought their dioceses have generally implemented the RCIA. They agreed at 88 percent, compared to 63 percent for those who have never implemented the RCIA (Table C42, Appendix C).

There were some regional differences among the priests on the early childhood question. The region that stands out most clearly is New England. Only 58 percent of the priests in New England thought that programs should start at a preschool level, compared to 79 percent of all priests (Table C42, Appendix C). Given the high interest among bishops and priests, there is a presumption that there will be an increased interest in the number of parishes that have preschool programs.

Unified Sacramental Programs

The unification of parish sacramental preparation programs is a source of contention in some parishes. Many religious educators seem to favor one parish program for all of the children and youth in the parish, including those who attend Catholic school. Many Catholic school administrators, teachers and parents think that the Catholic school is the best place for sacramental preparation for Catholic school students. If students have to go to a parish program as well as the Catholic school, that is seen as a duplication. The majority of bishops (69%) and priests (71%) agreed with the unified concept. They thought that sacramental preparation for eucharist, penance and confirmation should be given in one unified program (Table 19).

Those priests who had been a moderator of a parish religious education program believed in a unified program of sacramental preparation at a higher rate (75%) than those who had never been a moderator (65%), as did those who had implemented the RCIA (76% to 66%) (Table C43, Appendix C).

Children's Liturgy of the Word

Bishops and priests were almost evenly divided on whether there should be a separate children's liturgy of the word available in each parish every Sunday. Although children's liturgy of the word is a part of worship, as with the RCIA many parish religious educators staff that event. Therefore, it is a legitimate concern for religious educators.

For priests, age had a lot to do with whether or not they thought parishes should have a children's liturgy of the word available every Sunday. The younger priests were much more interested in children's liturgy of the word than the older priests (Table C44, Appendix C).

There were also distinct regional differences. Only 26 percent of the priests in the Great Lakes thought there should be children's liturgy of the word, whereas 65 percent of the priests in New England thought there should. Associates were more favorable (67%) than pastors (49%). Those priests who have never been in a parish with a school were very favorable (78%) compared to those who had (50%). Priests who are members of a religious community agreed at 64 percent compared to 49 percent for those who are not (Table C44, Appendix C).

Whether or not a parish has implemented the RCIA or a bishop perceives his diocese as having implemented the Rite also made a difference. Over 56 percent of all priests who have implemented the RCIA were in favor of children's liturgy or the word, compared to 44 percent for those who have not. Bishops had similar percentages (Table C44, Appendix C).

Summary

Bishops and priests definitely concurred that the diocese has the responsibility to ensure quality religious education programs in every parish and that parish programs operate best with strong support services from the diocese. They were, however, almost equally divided over whether the diocese should establish uniform programs in each parish.

There was no doubt that it is the pastor who has the overall responsibility for the parish program, including catechist formation. There was a strong perception, if not unanimity, that every parish needs a religious education board or committee.

Although they did not deny the importance of adult education, a very large percentage of the bishops and, to a slightly lesser extent, the priests did not think that the church should concentrate its efforts on adult religious education to the exclusion of children and youth. A solid majority of the bishops and again slightly fewer of the priests found the RCIA as the best hope for having knowledgeable and faith-filled Catholics in the future.

Most bishops and priests did agree that sacramental preparation programs that involve parents are the most common form of adult education. A majority also wanted sacramental preparation programs to become unified so that all children in the parish would attend the same program, including those in Catholic schools.

In regard to the future of religious education, three quarters of the bishops and priests said that family-centered programs offer the best hope. But slightly fewer thought that the church should move its catechetical programs in the family-centered direction.

Again, three quarters said that the church should concentrate its efforts on total youth ministry rather than on just religious education for youth, and an even higher number wanted every secondary program to include retreats.

Another solid majority wanted parish religious education programs to begin at the preschool level. The bishops and priests were split almost evenly over whether each parish should have at least one children's liturgy of the word every Sunday.

CHAPTER 5:

AGREEMENTS, DISAGREEMENTS, PATTERNS AND RELATIONSHIPS

Agreements

Bishops and priests were almost in unanimous agreement on a wide range of issues regarding religious education. Near unanimity is defined here as over 90 percent agreement by both groups. Knowing where the two groups agree can help parish leaders plan programs that fit the perceptions of the people ultimately responsible for the programs. Bishops and priests were nearly unanimous in the following areas.

Purpose and Value

Elementary and secondary programs perform an essential service for the church.They should cover a whole range of activities that engage people from early childhood throughout life and every parish should have programs that include activities for people of every age and stage of life. Their purposes are to help people grow in faith into mature adult Christians, to assist parents in their roles, to help participants understand and articulate why they are Catholic, and to help people to think critically about religion and society. They must also involve participants in learning doctrine, praying, serving, and experiencing community.

Bishops, but not the priests, judged that programs should help people become active Catholics, measured by regular participation in the sacramental life of the church.

Faith and Life

Every program should emphasize the relationship between faith and a person's life experience. To be authentically Catholic, programs must include social justice as a major dimension.

Effectiveness

In responding to questions on the effectiveness of current programs, bishops and priests disagreed among themselves. However, they did agree on the kinds of things they think make for successful programs.

Clearly written goals make programs more effective. For programs for children, it is essential that there be active support and involvement of parents. Every secondary program should include a regular retreat program. For any program to be successful, the pastor must be visibly supportive.

Bishops, but not priests, were nearly unanimous in saying written goals make it possible to evaluate programs and regular evaluations by parishioners help ensure that programs will improve. Bishops also were near unanimity in saying that Catholic schools are the best means of religious education for children and youth available to the church and that parish renewal programs like RENEW are effective adult catechetical programs and should be encouraged.

Responsibilities

Any parish program works best when it has strong support services from the diocese. In the parish, catechist training is an important responsibility of the pastor and the DRE.

Bishops were more convinced than priests that the diocese has the responsibility to ensure quality religious education programs in each parish, that the pastor has the overall responsibility for parish programs, and that a religious education board or committee is important to the parish program.

Content

Religious literacy should be a major goal of very program. Bishops were nearly unanimous in stating that a working knowledge of religious terms is important for a successful program. Both groups acknowledged that parish programs should always include study of the scriptures.

Disagreements

Bishops and priests disagreed on a narrower range of topics than they agreed. Yet their disagreements are instructive to the rest of the church since they probably reflect similar discussions that are taking place in parishes around the country. A disagreement is defined as less than 65 percent agreement on any statement.

Effectiveness

Both groups failed to agree on the effectiveness of the current structure of 30 weeks of classes each year. They also failed to agree whether or not it should be changed. There was no agreement either on whether parish programs are more cost effective than Catholic schools. Nor could they agree if program effectiveness for children and youth is directly related to the effectiveness of adult education.

As was the case with other issues, the bishops were more in agreement on effectiveness than were the priests. Priests could not agree on the relationship of funding to effectiveness, on whether elementary programs are more effective than secondary, and on how much help the universal catechism is likely to be in improving programs.

Responsibilities

There was great diversity of opinion over whether the diocese should establish uniform programs in each parish.

Specific Programs

There is no agreement about children's liturgy of the word being available in every parish. Priests were split over the RCIA as the best hope for having knowledgeable and faith-filled Catholics in the future and over Catholics schools being worthy of support and new ones built.

Patterns

Some patterns emerge from an analysis of the data. First, bishops are relatively homogeneous in their thinking. Perhaps that should be expected since the bishops are close to one another in age and members of an exclusive group among the clergy. Second, priests have many differences among them based on role, assignment, region, and whether or not they have implemented the RCIA. Below are some of the statistically significant differences found among the priests.

Pastors

Pastors were more likely to answer the questionnaire than associates. They were more inclined to say that in general parish programs were effective and that the classroom model of religious education is effective. Although the percentage difference is small, more pastors than other priests thought that the real purpose of religious education for children and youth is the effects it has on adult catechists and parents. At the same time they were less interested in the church's concentrating its efforts on adult education. Not as many pastors as associates saw sacramental preparation as the primary form of adult education.

Pastors were more favorable toward Catholic schools, but were less inclined to see parish program effectiveness tied to a professional DRE. They were also not as favorable toward family-centered catechesis or toward children's liturgy of the word.

Older Priests

Since most pastors are older than associates, it would be expected that the older clergy and the pastors would tend to agree on most issues. That was not the case. Only in their thinking that the purpose for religious education for young people is the effects it has on adults and in their lack of enthusiasm for children's liturgy did they agree.

The older clergy were more favorable toward family-centered catechesis and were more likely to say that programs have positive measurable effects. They thought the purpose of parish programs is instruction in the doctrines of the faith. They saw the universal catechism as being helpful in improving parish programs and they wanted to see those programs made uniform by the diocese. They were significantly less prone to say that the church should concentrate its efforts on adults. They were also the least likely to have implemented the RCIA.

Assignment

More priests who work in urban and suburban parishes have implemented the RCIA than have those in rural and inner city areas. They also saw the DRE as more important. Suburban priests were less in favor of family-centered catechesis; and suburban and inner city priests were stronger on the pastor's overall responsibility for parish programs.

Moderators of Parish Programs

Over 63 percent of the priests said that they have at one time or another been moderators or directors of parish religious education programs. Their thinking on some key issues is markedly different from other priests. They were more in favor of having a unified parish sacramental program, but had a lower percentage on the necessity of a professional DRE. They were not as inclined to think that programs have positive measurable effects, that social service programs were essential, or that the RCIA was the best hope for the future.

Regions

The New England priests stood out as unique in the country. More New England priests than those in any other area had attended at least some parish religious education. New England and the Mideast priests were the least interested in religious education boards or committees. New England priests (and bishops) showed the least enthusiasm for family-centered programs. New England priests had the lowest percentage of all regions in thinking that religious education should start in preschool.

New England and the Mideast were the least enthusiastic about the RCIA as the hope for the future and New England had the lowest number of parishes that had implemented the RCIA. However, New England priests were very much in favor of having children's liturgy of the word, while the Great Lakes region was the least in favor. New England and Southeast priests were less inclined to see schools as the best means for religious education available to the church.

Priests from the Mideast and West were the least likely to say that the most important part of religious education is instruction in the doctrines of the faith. The Mideast and the Great Lakes were less prone to say that parish programs were more cost effective than schools. The Mideast priests generally thought that the more funding the better the program.

RCIA

Of all of the areas under discussion, the implementation of the RCIA marks the greatest number of differences. Naturally those who have implemented the RCIA were more favorable toward it than those who have not. They were also more convinced that their parish programs are effective. They thought that for programs to be authentically Catholic they had to include social justice as a major dimension and that programs should include social service programs. They were more favorable toward religious education committees, were more likely to concentrate on adult education than on children and youth, and thought parish renewal programs should be encouraged.

They were less inclined to see regular evaluation tied to program effectiveness and to see the universal catechism as helping to improve parish programs. Along the same lines, they were less likely to see instruction in doctrine as a major purpose for religious education.

They thought that retreats should be a part of every secondary program and were more in favor of children's liturgy of the word. Finally, as a group they were less favorable toward Catholic schools.

Relationships

As mentioned earlier, the bishops were much more homogeneous than the priests. Their responses to questions were more within expected frequencies than priests. Also there were more statistically significant correlations among bishops' responses than among the priests'. Although it is important to remember that correlation is a statistic that describes a magnitude of relation, not causation, it is possible to gain some insights based on correlation coefficients from among the questions answered by bishops and priests.

Purpose and Content of Religious Education

Bishops who thought that a purpose of religious education is to help people become active Catholics as measured by Mass attendance and the reception of the sacraments also thought that the universal catechism would be a great help in improving parish programs, that the most important part of any program is instruction in the doctrines of the faith, and that the main purpose of religious education is to communicate sound doctrine to children and youth.

Those bishops who wanted programs to help participants understand and articulate why they are Catholic also wanted programs that involve parents, emphasize the relationship between faith and life experiences, and lead to prayer, service, and community. If bishops said that the purpose of religious education was to assist parents in their role, they also said that students should be involved in programs which lead to instruction in doctrine, prayer, service, and community. Bishops who thought that programs should include a social justice dimension thought that the students should participate in a social service program.

Bishops who were in favor of programs that include activities for people of every age saw all of the following: a religious education committee is important; written goals are a sign of effectiveness; the purpose of religious education is to help people grow in faith; programs should include the four-fold dimension; the involvement of parents is critical; programs must include a social justice dimension; students must participate in social service; and renewal programs are an effective form of adult education. Those who wanted total youth ministry programs also wanted to require social service programs.

There were far fewer relations among the priests' answers. Those priests who said that the most important part of any program is instruction in the doctrines of the faith also thought that the main purpose or religious education was to communicate sound doctrine, that the diocese should establish uniform programs, and that the classroom model should be changed. If priests thought the universal catechism would be helpful to the parish, they also thought that the main purpose of programs was to communicate doctrine. Those who said programs should help people articulate why they are Catholic thought that religious literacy should be a major goal of every program.

Like the bishops, priests who were convinced that there must be a social justice dimension in authentically Catholic programs thought that these same programs should require participation in social service. Further, these same priests perceived that a committee or board is an important part of any program, viewed renewal programs as effective forms of adult education, and wanted retreats as a part of secondary programs.

Effectiveness

In the area of effectiveness, there were fewer clear relationships than in purpose and content. Those bishops who thought more funding meant greater effectiveness thought that the most effective programs have a DRE; they would also require social service programs. For priests too there was a relationship between funding and a DRE.

Bishops who liked the current classroom structure thought the programs in their dioceses generally effective and in fact all religious education programs generally effective. The bishops who said programs have a measurable, positive effect also found programs generally effective. The priests who liked the classroom model also found programs generally effective. On the other hand, bishops who wanted to change the classroom model thought the church should concentrate on adult education rather than on children and youth.

Both bishops and priests who said that elementary religious education programs are more effective than secondary programs said, with great consistency, that secondary are not as effective as elementary.

If bishops said that the pastor must be visibly supportive of a program, they also said that parish programs operate best with strong diocesan support services. If they thought that program effectiveness was in direct proportion to the effectiveness of programs for adults, they were in favor of one unified sacramental program.

If bishops said that Catholic schools are the best means available to the church for religious education, they also said that more schools should be built. If they thought that parish programs were more cost effective than schools, they did not think that more schools should be built. In this case, the priests followed the thinking of the bishops with one addition. If they thought schools were the best means, they did not think religious education programs more cost effective than schools.

If priests perceived renewal programs positively, they also saw the value of a board or committee, regular evaluations, total youth ministry, and the RCIA.

Structure

For bishops, there was a connection between thinking that parish programs operate best with strong support from the diocese and thinking that the purpose of the program is to help people grow into mature Christians. For the priests, diocesan support was connected to diocesan responsibility for ensuring quality programs in each parish and goals being a part of effective programs.

In a high degree of consistency, the bishops who thought that family-centered catechesis offers the best hope for the future also wanted to move all programs toward that model. They also wanted a unified sacramental preparation program and would require social service. The priests were as consistent as the bishops in their views on family-centered catechesis.

CHAPTER 6:
CONCLUSIONS

Data do not produce conclusions. Only people can draw conclusions based on subjective judgment. Even if presented simply and with as much objectivity as possible, conclusions are always subjective; they are produced by a subject. No matter how carefully the material is presented, there is a certain skewing based on, if nothing else, what has been omitted. Yet, it is the inferences, the insights, and the summation of the data that are most useful in any study. With these cautions, it is possible to draw some conclusions.

Bishops and Priests

A common topic of discussion within the church is the graying of the American clergy. Although the bishops and priests are not young, their average ages are not unusually high for men in this country in management positions. Bishops at 60 and priests at 52 are not as old on average as the informal discussion would indicate. However, given the low replacement rate for priests, that average age is expected to rise.

It is no surprise that large numbers of bishops and priests went to Catholic schools. What was a surprise is that over one quarter of the clergy participated in a parish religious education program at some time in their youth.

Some mildly surprising information is that one in three priests minister in rural areas of the country. More than one out of every four bishops have never been pastors of a parish. Yet over half of the bishops and 60 percent of the priests have been moderators of parish religious education programs.

The uneven spread of the RCIA around the country was also a source of mild astonishment. The low rates of implementation in the northern area of the east coast was unexpected.

Purposes of Religious Education

If bishops and priests were clear on one thing it was the goals of parish programs. They saw these programs as essential to the church and they want programs that contain the four-fold sign of Catholic education: message, worship, service, and community (NCD, 1979, #213). They saw the purposes as helping people grow in the faith into mature adult Christians who can articulate why they are Catholic. For programs for children and youth, a major purpose is to help parents in their role as educators of their children. Many bishops and priests wanted parish programs to begin at the preschool level.

As was seen earlier, they did not hesitate to make the connection between belief and daily living. They wanted programs that relate to all ages. For people to be justly served by religious education, they thought they must be taught to think critically about religion and society and that they must be taught about social justice.

None of those ideas is new. They are all contained in one way or another in church documents. What the bishops and priests said was that they agreed with those documents and saw the importance of what the church has taught.

Content

The intellectual content of religious education was not a source of disagreement. Bishops and priests wanted Catholics who are religiously literate about the content of the faith and about the scriptures. Many of them were not willing to say that "the main purpose of religious education is to communicate sound doctrine to children and youth." Given their insistence on the connection between faith and life, that stance is consistent. They were not denying the value of doctrine, but insisting on more than intellectual assent.

A large number of priests did not see the universal catechism as offering much help for the parish; they know that a catechism alone does not make a parish program effective. Being further removed from the parish, bishops were more optimistic.

Effectiveness

Bishops and priests were in general agreement about some of the signs of effective parish programs. These programs should have clearly written goals, support and involvement from parents, visible support from the pastor, and regular, parishioner-based evaluation procedures. Many acknowledged the essential value to a parish of a professional DRE. They were split over the proportional relationship of money to effectiveness. They named elementary programs more effective than secondary.

One of the greatest sources of contention came over the perceived effectiveness of the most common parish program for children and youth. Over 60 percent of the clergy said that the current structure of one hour (more or less) per week for 30 weeks per year is not effective. Yet 75 percent of the bishops and over 50 percent of the priests said that kind of program should not be changed. Such a response might be understood in the context of a fear of innovation and experimentation, a valid concern in such an important area. But to say something does not work and then say it should not be changed is at best illogical.

To further compound the issue, three quarters of the bishops and priests said that although they could be improved, in general parish programs are effective and that the programs in their dioceses or their parishes are effective. That response does not mean that a majority of parishes does not have the "classroom" model, the thirty hours per year. It means rather that many bishops and priests have not crystallized their own thinking on this crucial matter.

The bishops and priests have not changed their collective mind on the question of schools since they were last surveyed almost two years ago. Bishops slightly more than priests saw schools as the best means available to the church for religious education and many bishops, although not so many priests, wanted new schools built.

Responsibilities

The responsibility question was: Whose job is religious education? There was no doubt that the overall responsibility for parish programs rests with the pastor. He shares that responsibility with the DRE and the religious education board or committee if they exist. The job of the diocese was seen as ensuring quality control and offering support services to the parishes. It is not the job of the diocese, according to half of the bishops and a majority of the priests, to mandate uniform programs in every parish.

Adult Education

Adult education is obviously important to the clergy, but not so important that it should be the sole emphasis. They wanted a catechetical commitment from the church for all of its members, adults, youth, and children. They were very favorable toward parish renewal programs such as RENEW because they recognized them as effective forms of adult catechesis. The bishops were more enthusiastic than the priests about the RCIA as a great hope for the future.

Since they were very much in favor of programs for all ages, it would not be rash to think that bishops and priests would be almost unanimous in favoring family-centered programs. Yet they were split on whether all programs should move in that direction. It is possible that bishops' and priests' understanding of the meaning of family-centered religious education may not have been consistent. Even though over 70 percent of the clergy were in favor of family-centered programs, they may not all have meant the same thing.

Children and Youth

The question of program effectiveness for secondary students would seem to warrant a move toward total youth ministry. The clergy seemed to agree with that direction by strongly supporting retreats as a part of secondary programs. But when faced with the question directly, only three in four concurred. It is not clear why they would not be more in favor of comprehensive programs for teenagers.

A thorny issue in many parishes connected to schools is the sacramental preparation program. A majority of bishops and priests favored one unified program for children in schools and religious education, but not by anything approaching unanimity. Although it is not perceived as a particularly controversial issue, they were split right down the middle on children's liturgy of the word.

Reflections

Given the above data, the church knows some things about what bishops and priests say about the church's catechetical ministry. It is what the church does not know about that ministry that causes concern.

Bishops and priests were generally very supportive of the church's catechetical efforts, as they should be. They were not convinced, however, that the programs for children and youth are effective. This basic contradiction indicates some illogical ways of thinking about catechesis.

That kind of thinking says that if something is done with good intentions it is good. Hundreds of thousands of people give generously of their time and energy to help the church fulfill its catechetical mission. Yet the church knows almost nothing with any certitude about the quality of religious education programs in this country.

In the USCC study of the studies of religious education mentioned earlier, Mahoney (1987) correctly pointed out that the lack of a comprehensive scientific study on catechesis does not mean that it is impossible to have any understanding of the effectiveness of catechesis in the United States (p. 2). Although anecdotal evidence gives some understanding, only scientific evidence motivates people to invest the kinds of money, time, and energy that programs need.

Mahoney also pointed out several times the "uneven quality of the research studies" included in his report and the lack of empirical evidence for effectiveness (p.3). A careful reading of the study confirms his comment that "Catholic schools remain one of the few areas which have been subjected to constant critical evaluation by both those within and those outside that particular form of ministry" (p. 4). Almost every empirical study quoted by Mahoney pertains to Catholic schools.

The sad truth is that the Catholic church in the United States has little knowledge about its catechetical programs. The church does not know how many children, youth, and adults participate. The last serious study for elementary and secondary students was published by Thompson and Hemrick (1982) and they admit that their figures were not highly reliable (pp. 16-17). Since then, the church has had to guess at the numbers.

Even when it guesses, people disagree about what those guesses mean. Some say that the figures are too low because the data gathering techniques are faulty. Some say they are far too high because they represent enrollment, not actual attendance. Just because someone is enrolled in a program does not mean that the person is there every session or even most of the sessions.

This kind of question is not just a national concern. Many dioceses do not know the numbers of students, the numbers of teachers, or the kinds of materials they are using. Without basic data, it is difficult to plan or in fact to discuss anything meaningfully.

A major concern is the quality of teaching, something that many suspect is tied directly to the presence of a professional DRE. The key word is "suspect" since there is no scientific evidence either way. At the present time, there are something like 2,500 professional parish DREs in the country, with approximately 2,000 additional nonprofessionals acting in this capacity. In spite of conceptually strong support from bishops and priests, the general impression is that the numbers of professional DREs are decreasing. The job has little room for advancement. The pay is low. And job security is often dependent on the current pastor. Few people, it seems, are entering the field.

Many pastors use part-time, stipended people as coordinators of religious education and find that the program goes on as usual. What they also find is that after one or two years the program begins to slip. Only a professional has the skills to do teacher training and curriculum development. In the long run, only a professional DRE can inspire confidence in parents.

To get back to the quality of teaching, no one knows the values and beliefs of the catechists or of the students. The religious education department of the NCEA has developed the tools, but no one has used them scientifically. No one has done an empirical study to see if the catechists believe what the church believes. No one has done a scientific study to see if the students learn anything or to see if what they may learn makes any difference in their lives.

In line with what Mahoney said earlier, some correctly say that scientific knowledge is not the only kind of knowledge. They point out that many adult behaviors do not come from the way people think, but how they feel. That argument would be more persuasive if there were some general agreement, let alone consensus, on the form catechetical ministry should take in the church. There is no consensus, because there is no knowledge. No one knows what programs have the most positive effects on adult behaviors. The adult behaviors are known, but not the connections.

Most people would agree that there are successful programs. Some have even tried to identify them. However, from a scientific point of view, no one knows what they really look like or where they are. It would be very helpful if those programs could be identified as models for other parishes.

There is even less information about catechesis to special groups, such as the Hispanic community. If, as many people say, half of the church in the United States will be Hispanic within 15 to 20 years, it would be helpful to the church's ministry to know something about their catechetical needs.

There is no question about the dedication of all the people involved in parish religious education programs—catechists, pastors, DREs, parents. The question is: how can the church best accomplish its catechetical mission? For all of the resources that go into catechesis, the church owes it to its members to do a comprehensive, longitudinal scientific study of the church's total catechetical ministry. Such a study would provide the basis for planning for the future of catechesis which would allow dioceses and parishes to ensure quality religious education programs for all age groups in the church. It would also provide bishops and priests with the insights necessary for the bold and persistent leadership so needed in this age.

APPENDIX A:

RESEARCH METHODOLOGY

Instrument

With the help of a panel of experts composed of eight people in the field, the author developed the survey instrument in 1987; that development included validity and reliability studies. A pilot study was conducted with 35 randomly selected priests from the Diocese of Richmond. The return from that study was 100 percent. The questionnaire proved reliable and the priests were invited to comment on the questionnaire in general and on individual questions to help with validity.

There were two instruments in the study, one for bishops and one for priests. Part I of each contained twelve items concerning background data for the respondent similar to the questions in the *Mixed Messages* questionnaire. Part I of the two questionnaires differed slightly for each group.

Part II contained 53 items related to the (1) purpose and value, (2) effectiveness, and (3) structure of parish religious education program. The bishop and priest respondents were asked to give current perceptions for each item according to a four-point scale: strongly agree, agree, disagree, strongly disagree. For the purposes of reporting and discussion, the data were collapsed from four categories to two: agreed and disagreed. Part II of the questionnaire was the same for both groups. Copies of the questionnaire can be found in Appendix B.

Subjects

Of the total population of 276 active Roman Catholic bishops in the United States, 200, or 72.5 percent, responded. The large response rate was due in part to a letter from John R. Roach, the Archbishop of St. Paul and Minneapolis (see Appendix B). A postage-paid envelope was included in each letter. Two follow-up letters were sent after the initial questionnaire to those who had not responded.

According to the publisher of *The Official Catholic Directory*, there were 18,489 pastors and 20,350 parochial vicars or associates in the United States at the time of the mailing. The questionnaire was sent to a random sample of 655 priests. The mailing list was generated by the publishers of *The Official Catholic Directory* and contained a label for every fifty-sixth priest, beginning with a randomly-selected first number. For the purposes of this study, a random sample size of 655 was an adequate number (Hinkle and Oliver, 1983).

The response rate for priests was 47.2 percent, 309 returns out of 655 sent. The responses were validated by contacting 30 randomly-selected priests from those who did not respond to the original questionnaire.

The reliability for the bishops' responses is plus or minus three percent at the .05 level of confidence. For the priests, it is plus or minus four percent at the .05 level of confidence.

A small number of respondents, five bishops and six priests commented on various topics on the questionnaire itself. Three noted the difficulty in obtaining precise data from any kind of questionnaire. One bishop complained that the questionnaire treated the parish "as if it were some sort of uniform and homogeneous grouping of people. This simply isn't the case." One priest said that the questions "went to the heart of the matter" and dealt with "the real issues."

Treatment of Data

The SPSSx and SAS were used to determine the basic characteristics of the data. A chi-square treatment tested the statistical significance between the expected and observed frequencies. The study accepted levels of significance of .05. The Pearson correlation coefficient was used to determine if there were any significant correlations among items. The study reported correlations of +_.30 at the .001 or above confidence level. Complete tables of all of the responses are available from the author.

APPENDIX B:

QUESTIONNAIRES AND LETTERS

A STUDY OF THE PERCEPTIONS OF BISHOPS TOWARD PARISH RELIGIOUS EDUCATION PROGRAMS

PART I

Directions: Numbers 1-12 are items of background information. Please be as accurate as possible. For each question, please **insert** the correct number or circle the number which corresponds to your answer.

1. What is your age?

 ____

2. How long have you been ordained a priest?

 ____

3. How long have you been ordained a bishop?

 ____

4. What is your present role?
 1. diocesan bishop
 2. auxiliary bishop
 3. retired bishop

5. Did you attend a Catholic elementary school?
 1. did not attend
 2. 1-2 years
 3. 3-4 years
 4. 5-8 years

6. Did you attend a Catholic high school?
 1. did not attend
 2. 1-2 years
 3. 3-4 years

7. Did you attend a parish religious education program (besides a Catholic school)?
 1. did not attend
 2. 1-2 years
 3. 3-4 years
 4. 5-8 years
 5. 9 years or more

8. What portion of your ministry has been in a parish with a school?
 1. none
 2. 1-5 years
 3. 6-10 years
 4. 11 years or more

9. How many years were you the pastor of a parish?
 1. none
 2. 1-3 years
 3. 4-6 years
 4. 7 years or more

10. Were you ever the moderator or director of a parish religious education program?
 1. yes
 2. no

11. Were you ever a full time teacher or administrator of a Catholic school?
 1. yes
 2. no

12. In general, have the parishes in your (arch)diocese implemented the Rite of Christian Initiation of Adults (RCIA)?
 1. yes
 2. no

(Please continue to Part II)

PART II

Directions: Items 13-65 represent points of view about religious education programs. Using the following scale, please indicate your reaction to these statements by **circling** the appropriate abbreviation following each item.

SA = STRONGLY AGREE
A = AGREE
D = DISAGREE
SD = STRONGLY DISAGREE

Please note that the questions do not refer to Catholic school religious education programs unless they are specifically mentioned.

13.	Elementary and secondary parish religious education programs (CCD) perform an essential service for the church.	13.	SA	A	D	SD
14.	Religious education programs should teach people to think critically about religion and society.	14.	SA	A	D	SD
15.	In general, the more funding available to religious education programs the more effective they will be.	15.	SA	A	D	SD
16.	The most effective religious education programs have a paid, full time professional director of religious education (DRE).	16.	SA	A	D	SD
17.	The purpose of parish religious education programs for children is to assist parents in their roles as those primarily and principally responsible for the education of their children.	17.	SA	A	D	SD
18.	The universal catechism being prepared by the Holy See will be a great help in improving parish religious education programs.	18.	SA	A	D	SD
19.	Religious education programs that have clear written goals are more effective than those that do not.	19.	SA	A	D	SD
20.	A religious education board or committee is an important part of any parish religious education program.	20.	SA	A	D	SD
21.	The main purpose of religious education is to help people grow in the faith into mature adult Christians.	21.	SA	A	D	SD
22.	Parish religious education programs should emphasize the relationship between faith and one's life experience.	22.	SA	A	D	SD
23.	The current structure for parish religious education programs, that is, a one to one and one-half hour class for approximately 30 weeks per year, is effective.	23.	SA	A	D	SD
24.	A parish religious education program operates best with strong support services from the (arch)diocese.	24.	SA	A	D	SD
25.	A purpose of religious education is to help people become active Catholics, measured by regular Mass attendance and the reception of the sacraments.	25.	SA	A	D	SD
26.	The most important part of any religious education program is instruction in the doctrines of the faith.	26.	SA	A	D	SD
27.	Religious education programs that have regular ways for parishioners to evaluate and improve them are more effective than those who do not.	27.	SA	A	D	SD
28.	Catechist training is an important responsibility of the pastor and the professional religious educator.	28.	SA	A	D	SD
29.	In order to be considered successful, religious education should help participants understand and articulate why they are Catholic.	29.	SA	A	D	SD
30.	The religious education programs in my diocese are generally effective.	30.	SA	A	D	SD
31.	In order for a parish program to be successful, the pastor must be visibly supportive of all aspects of the program.	31.	SA	A	D	SD
32.	In order to be considered successful, religious education should help participants attain a working knowledge of religious terms.	32.	SA	A	D	SD
33.	The current elementary "classroom" or "school model" used in many parish religious education programs should be changed.	33.	SA	A	D	SD
34.	The pastor has the overall responsibility for the parish religious education program.	34.	SA	A	D	SD
35.	Parish religious education should encompass a whole range of programs and activities that engage the Catholic throughout life, beginning with early childhood.	35.	SA	A	D	SD
36.	Besides involving participants in doctrine, religious education programs should lead them to prayer, service, and an experience of community.	36.	SA	A	D	SD
37.	Catholic schools are the best means for the religious education of children and youth available to the church.	37.	SA	A	D	SD
38.	Parish religious education programs should include activities for people in every age and stage of life.	38.	SA	A	D	SD

39.	The (arch)diocese has the responsibility to ensure quality religious education programs in each parish.	39.	SA	A	D	SD
40.	The main purpose of religious education is to communicate sound doctrine to children and youth.	40.	SA	A	D	SD
41.	Parish religious education programs for children and youth are more cost effective than Catholic schools.	41.	SA	A	D	SD
42.	All parish religious education programs should move toward the model of family-centered catechesis.	42.	SA	A	D	SD
43.	In order to be authentically Catholic, religious education must include social justice as a major dimension.	43.	SA	A	D	SD
44.	Elementary and secondary parish religious education programs have measurable, positive effects on adult Catholic religious behavior.	44.	SA	A	D	SD
45.	The real purpose for the church's having religious education programs for children and youth is the effects it has on adult catechists and parents.	45.	SA	A	D	SD
46.	In most parishes, the sacramental preparation program for parents is the most common form of adult education.	46.	SA	A	D	SD
47.	Every parish religious education program for secondary students should include a systematic retreat program.	47.	SA	A	D	SD
48.	The (arch)diocese should establish uniform religious education programs in each parish.	48.	SA	A	D	SD
49.	Parish religious education should always include scripture study.	49.	SA	A	D	SD
50.	Family-centered religious education offers the best hope for the future of religious education.	50.	SA	A	D	SD
51.	The church should concentrate its efforts on adult religious education, rather than on children and youth.	51.	SA	A	D	SD
52.	Parish religious education programs for children and youth should require the participants to participate in a social service program.	52.	SA	A	D	SD
53.	The active support and involvement of parents are critical for parish religious education programs for children.	53.	SA	A	D	SD
54.	The church should concentrate its efforts on total youth ministry rather than on just religious education efforts for youth.	54.	SA	A	D	SD
55.	Religious literacy should be a major goal of every religious education program.	55.	SA	A	D	SD
56.	Parish renewal programs, for example, RENEW, are effective adult catechetical programs and should be encouraged.	56.	SA	A	D	SD
57.	Because it involves so many people in the parish, the Rite of Christian Initiation of Adults (RCIA) is the best hope for having knowledgeable and faith- filled Catholics in the future.	57.	SA	A	D	SD
58.	Elementary religious education programs are more effective than secondary programs.	58.	SA	A	D	SD
59.	Given the church's commitment to religious education, Catholic schools should be supported and new ones built.	59.	SA	A	D	SD
60.	Secondary religious education programs are just as effective as elementary.	60.	SA	A	D	SD
61.	Sacramental preparation for eucharist, penance, and confirmation should be given in one unified program for all children and youth of a given parish, whether they are in Catholic school or not.	61.	SA	A	D	SD
62.	The effectiveness of parish religious education programs for children and youth is in direct proportion to the effectiveness of parish programs for adults.	62.	SA	A	D	SD
63.	Parish religious education programs should begin at the pre-school level.	63.	SA	A	D	SD
64.	Although they could be improved, parish religious education programs are generally effective.	64.	SA	A	D	SD
65.	A separate children's liturgy of the word should be available at least at one eucharist every Sunday in every parish.	65.	SA	A	D	SD

Comments: ____

____

____

____

A STUDY OF THE PERCEPTIONS OF PARISH PRIESTS TOWARD PARISH RELIGIOUS EDUCATION PROGRAMS

PART I

Directions: Numbers 1-12 are items of background information. Please be as accurate as possible. For each question, please **insert** the correct number or circle the number which corresponds to your answer.

1. What is your age?

   ____

2. How long have you been ordained a priest?

   ____

3. What is your present role?
   1. pastor
   2. non-pastor, but primarily involved in parish work
   3. parish team ministry
   4. primarily involved in non-parish work

4. Did you attend a Catholic elementary school?
   1. did not attend
   2. 1-2 years
   3. 3-4 years
   4. 5-8 years

5. Did you attend a Catholic high school?
   1. did not attend
   2. 1-2 years
   3. 3-4 years

6. Did you attend a parish religious education program (besides a Catholic school)?
   1. did not attend
   2. 1-2 years
   3. 3-4 years
   4. 5-8 years
   5. 9 years or more

7. What portion of your ministry has been in a parish with a school?
   1. none
   2. 1-5 years
   3. 6-10 years
   4. 11 years or more

8. In which area would you classify your present assignment?
   1. **inner city:**
      an area with a major city generally located within the central portion and having a large concentration of low income inhabitants.
   2. **urban but not inner city:**
      located within the limits of a major city, but not within an area designated as the inner city.
   3. **suburban:**
      located outside of the limits of a major city.
   4. **small town or rural:**
      located in an area that is not considered a suburb.

9. Were you ever the moderator or director of a parish religious education program?
   1. yes
   2. no

10. Were you ever a full time teacher or administrator of a Catholic school?
    1. yes
    2. no

11. Are you a member of a religious community?
    1. yes
    2. no

12. Has your parish implemented the Rite of Christian Initiation of Adults (RCIA)?
    1. yes
    2. no

(Please continue to Part II)

January 13, 1988

Your Excellency:

I need your help -- less than 20 minutes of your time!

I am conducting a national study on the perceptions of United States bishops and priests toward parish religious education programs. You have been selected to participate in this study. Because of your generosity in the past, I know I can count on your assistance.

Please complete the enclosed survey and return it to me in the enclosed envelope before Friday, February 5, 1988.

Let me assure you that this survey is anonymous. All responses are completely confidential. None of the data will be reported in such a way that any individual can be identified.

Thank you for your help. May the Lord bless you in your work.

Sincerely,

Stephen O'Brien

Reverend J. Stephen O'Brien
Executive Director
Department of Chief Administrators

Encl:

(The letter to the priests was essentially the same as the one to the bishops.)

Suite 100, 1077 30th Street, NW, Washington, DC 20007-3852 • (202) 337-6232

January 11, 1988

Your Excellency:

As chairman of the board of directors of the National Catholic Educational Association, I would encourage you to respond to the enclosed survey on parish religious education programs. I know the many demands on your time but I also know of your generosity.

I hope that the few minutes you will spend in answering these questions will benefit religious education in our country.

Thank you for considering this request. With best personal wishes, I am

Sincerely Yours in Christ,

Most Reverend John R. Roach, D.D.
Archbishop of Saint Paul and Minneapolis
Chairman, NCEA Board of Directors

Suite 100, 1077 30th Street, NW, Washington, DC 20007-3852 • (202) 337-6232

APPENDIX C:

TABLES

Table C1 - Present Role

Role of Priests	Respondents %
Pastor	59
Associate	22
Team Ministry	3
Non-parish	16
Member of Religious Community	25
Role of Bishops	
Diocesan bishop	71
Auxiliary	27
Retired	2

Table C2 - Priests' Role by Membership in Religious Communities

Role	Respondents Priests %
Pastor	43
Associate	19
Team ministry	3
Non-parish	35

Table C3 - Years in Parish with a School

	Respondents							
	None		1 - 5		6 - 10		11 or more	
	Bshps %	Prsts %	Bshps %	Prst %	Bshps %	Prsts %	Bshps %	Prsts %
Age								
35 and under	-	10	-	6	-	24	-	0
36 - 45	-	10	-	30	-	21	-	40
46 - 55	10	9	44	22	38	14	8	55
56 - 65	5	10	26	12	21	15	49	63
65 and over	5	4	25	4	20	7	49	85

Because of averaging, rows do not always equal 100

Table C4 - Full Time Catholic School Experience by Years Ordained Priest

	Respondents	
	Bishops %	Priests %
Years Ordained		
10 and under	-	24
11 - 20	20	38
21 - 30	54	45
31 - 40	31	48
41 and over	47	62

Table C5 - States by NCEA Regions

Regions	States
New England	Connecticut, Maine, Massachusetts, New Hampshire, Rhode Island, Vermont
Mideast	Delaware, District of Columbia, Maryland, New Jersey, New York, Pennsylvania
Great Lakes	Illinois, Indiana, Michigan, Ohio, Wisconsin, Iowa, Kansas, Minnesota, Missouri, Nebraska, North Dakota, South Dakota
Southeast	Alabama, Arkansas, Florida, Georgia, Kentucky, Louisiana, Mississippi, North Carolina, South Carolina, Tennessee, Virginia, West Virginia
West	Alaska, Arizona, California, Colorado, Hawaii, Idaho, Montana, Nevada, New Mexico, Oklahoma, Oregon, Texas, Utah, Washington, Wyoming

Table C6 - Priests Attended Parish Religious Education by Region

	Respondents Priests %			
	None	1 - 4	5 - 8	9 or more
Regions				
New England	52	19	19	10
Mideast	73	12	7	8
Great Lakes	83	10	6	0
Plains	83	8	3	8
Southeast	74	6	6	13
West	72	4	9	15

Table C7 - Implemented RCIA

	Respondents	
	Bishops %	Priests %
Regions		
New England	42	43
Mideast	71	43
Great Lakes	88	71
Plains	65	54
Southeast	91	85
West	80	63
Age		
35 and under		67
36 - 45		70
46 - 55		62
56 - 65		56
66 and over		39
Assessment		
Inner City		49
Urban		73
Suburban		70
Rural		44

Table C8 - Priests' Perceptions about Programs Helping People Become Active Catholics by Years Ordained Priest

	Priests Agreed %
Years Ordained	
10 and under	86
11 - 20	79
21 - 30	90
31 - 40	85
41 and over	100

Table C9 - Priests' Perceptions about Purpose as Communication of Sound Doctrine to Children and Youth

	Priests Agreed %
Region	
New England	71
Mideast	71
Great Lakes	65
Plains	65
Southwest	88
West	56
Role	
Pastor	71
Associate	71
Team Ministry	30
Non-parish	65
Full time teacher or administrator	75
No full time school experience	63
Implemented RCIA	62
Have not implemented	79

Table C10 - Perceptions of the Purpose of Religious Education Being Effects on Catechists and Parents

	Bishops Agreed %
Moderator of Religious Education	20
Not moderator	9

	Priests Agreed %
Years Ordained	
10 and under	15
11 - 20	18
21 - 30	29
31 - 40	18
41 and over	51

Role	Priests Agreed %
Pastor	27
Associate	17
Team	50
Non-parish	14

Table C11 - Bishops' Perceptions Encompassing a Range of Activities Throughout Life

	Bishops Agreed %
Moderator of Religious Education	97
Not moderator	89

Table C12 - Bishops' Perceptions of Programs Helping People to Think Critically

	Bishops Agreed %
Years Ordained	
10 and under	-
11 - 20	100
21 - 30	98
31 - 40	89
41 and over	98

Table C13 - Priests' Perceptions of Participants Having Knowledge of Religious Terms

Role	Priests Agreed %
Pastor	87
Associate	84
Team Ministry	100
Non-parish	98

Table C14 - Priests' Perceptions that Instruction in Doctrine is Most Important

	Priest Agreed %
Age	
35 and under	61
36 - 45	58
46 - 55	66
56 - 65	70
65 and over	84
Role	
Pastor	70
Associate	66
Team Ministry	20
Non-parish	71
Region	
New England	77
Mideast	76
Great Lakes	59
Plains	68
Southeast	79
West	56
Implemented	62
Not Implemented RCIA	74
Attended parish religious education	62
Did not attend	81

Table C15 - Priests' Perceptions of Universal Catechism as Helping

	Priests Agreed %
Age	
35 and under	44
36 - 45	57
46 - 55	51
56 - 65	67
66 and over	93
Implemented RCIA	60
Not Implemented RCIA	72

Table C16: Perceptions that Programs for Children and Youth Require Participation in Social Service.

	Respondents	
	Bishops Agreed %	Priests Agreed %
Region		
New England	67	
Mideast	70	
Great Lakes	90	
Plains	100	
Southeast	84	
West	84	
Full-time Catholic School	91	
Never Full-time	78	
Implemented RCIA	87	81
Not Implemented RCIA	74	68
Moderator of Religious Education		72
Never Moderator		83

Table C17: Elementary and Secondary Programs' Measurable Effects

	Respondents	
	Bishops Agreed %	Priests Agreed %
Parishes Implemented RCIA	87	
Not Implemented	74	
Age		
35 and under		59
36 - 45		79
46 - 55		78
56 - 65		81
66 and over		84
Moderator of Religious Education		74
Never Moderator		85

Table C18: Bishops' Perceptions of Elementary Programs As More Effective Than Secondary

	Bishops Agreed %
Age	
35 and under	
36 - 45	50
46 - 55	61
56 - 65	83
65 and over	75

Table C19: Priests' Perception of Elementary Programs As More Effective Than Secondary

	Priests Agreed %
Years Ordained	
10 and under	44
11 - 20	66
21 - 30	64
31 - 40	69
41 and over	67
Regions	
New England	41
Mideast	74
Great Lakes	62
Plains	71
Southeast	63
West	54
Years in Parish With School	
None	30
1 - 5	59
6 - 10	61
11 or more	70
Attended Catholic Secondary School	66
Never Attended	49
Member of Religious Community	52
Not a member	66

Table C20: Secondary Programs Just As Effective As Elementary

	Respondents	
	Bishops Agreed %	Priests Agreed %
Worked Full-time in Catholic School	26	
Never Worked Full-time	47	
Attended Secondary School		31
Never Attended		41
Years in Parish with School		
None		65
1 - 5		36
6 - 10		31
11 or more		27

Table C21: Parish Renewal Programs As Effective and Should Be Encouraged

Years Ordained Priest	
10 and under	91
11 - 20	84
21 - 30	83
31 - 40	79
41 and over	63
Implemented RCIA	85
Not Implemented RCIA	75

Table C22: Program Effectiveness for Children and Youth in Direct Proportion to Adult Program Effectiveness

	Respondent	
	Bishops Agreed %	Priests Agreed %
Parishes Implemented RCIA	45	
Not Implemented RCIA	21	
Years in Parish With School		
None		78
1 - 5		49
6 - 10		40
11 or more		35
Member of Religious Community		59
Not a Member		37

Table C23: Priests' Perceptions of Programs With Regular Ways for Parishioners to Evaluate As More Effective

	Priests Agreed %
Assignment	
Inner City	77
Urban	93
Suburban	88
Rural	82
Implemented RCIA	92
Not Implemented	78

Table C24: Bishops' Perception of Most Effective Programs Having DREs

	Bishops Agreed %
Full-time in Catholic School	89
Never Full-time	75

Table C25: Priests' Perceptions of Most Effective Programs Having DREs

	Priests Agreed %
Role	
Pastor	72
Associate	89
Team Ministry	100
Non-Parish	85
Assignment	
Inner City	73
Urban	80
Suburban	89
Rural	72
Attended Religious Education	
1 - 4	82
5 - 8	74
9 years or more	58
None	80
Years in Parish With School	
None	89
1 - 5	87
6 - 10	71
11 or more	75
Implemented RCIA	84
Never Implemented	68
Moderator of Religious Education	73
Never Moderator	86

Table C26: The More Funding, The More Effective the Program

	Respondents	
	Bishops Agreed %	Priests Agreed %
Years Ordained Priest		
10 and under	-	
11 - 20	80	
21 - 30	75	
31 - 40	58	
41 and over	79	
Region		
New England		53
Mideast		79
Great Lakes		53
Plains		60
Southeast		58
West		57

Table C27: Priests' Perceptions of Current Structure for Parish Programs As Effective

	Priests Agreed %
Years Ordained	
10 and under	18
11 - 20	38
21 - 30	41
31 - 40	51
40 and over	56
Role	
Pastor	47
Associate	29
Team Ministry	33
Non-Parish	36
Years in Parish With School	
None	58
1 - 5	28
6 - 10	36
11 or more	47

Table C28: Priests' Perceptions That Current Model Should Be Changed

	Priests Agreed %
Years Ordained Priest	
10 or under	53
11 - 20	52
21 - 30	54
31 - 40	36
41 or over	25
Full-time in Catholic School	37
Not Full-time	52

Table C29: Programs in Diocese or Parish Are Generally Effective

	Respondents	
	Bishops Agreed %	Priests Agreed %
Years Pastor		
None	79	
1 - 3	59	
4 - 6	86	
7 or more	85	
Role		
Pastor		84
Associate		73
Team Ministry		70
Non-Parish		47
Implemented RCIA		82
Not Implemented		72
Member of Religious Community		68
Not Member		80

Table C30: Priests Perceptions of Programs In General As Effective

	Priests Agreed %
Role	
Pastor	78
Associate	65
Team Ministry	50
Non-Parish	64
Years in Parish With School	
None	80
1 - 5	63
6 - 10	62
11 or more	79

Table C31: Priests' Perceptions of Programs for Children and Youth As More Cost Effective Than Catholic Schools

	Priests Agreed %
Years Ordained	
10 and under	51
11 - 20	55
21 - 30	51
31 - 40	43
41 and over	20
Regions	
New England	46
Mideast	34
Great lakes	42
Plains	45
Southeast	59
West	65
Attended Catholic Elementary School	
Not Attended	53
1 - 4	50
5 - 8	45

Table C32: Catholic Schools As Best Means For Religious Education of Children and Youth

	Priests Agreed %
Years Ordained	
10 and under	73
11 - 20	55
21 - 30	71
31 - 40	72
40 and over	89
Role	
Pastor	74
Associate	69
Team Ministry	30
Non-Parish	68
Regions	
New England	56
Mideast	78
Great Lakes	78
Plains	87
Southeas	66
West	47
Years in Parish With School	
None	48
1 - 5	68
6 - 10	66
11 or more	76
Full-time Catholic School	76
Not Full-time	66
Implemented RCIA	66
Not Implemented	77

Table C33: Priests' Perception That Diocese Should Establish Uniform Programs

	Priests Agreed %
Age	
35 and under	34
36 - 45	33
46 - 55	38
56 - 65	42
66 and over	60

Table C34: Priests' Perception that Pastor Has An Overall Responsibility for the Program

	Priests Agreed %
Assignment	
Inner City	97
Urban	85
Suburban	93
Rural	83

Table C35: Board or Committee As an Important Part of a Parish Program

	Respondents	
	Bishops Agreed %	Priests Agreed %
Regions		
New England	77	68
Mideast	82	75
Great Lakes	90	86
Plains	100	88
Southeast	100	94
West	96	83
Implemented RCIA		85
Not Implemented		77

Table C36: Priests' Perceptions of Church's Concentrating Its Efforts On Adult Religious Education

	Priests Agreed %
Age	
35 and under	43
36 - 45	29
46 - 55	39
56 - 65	24
65 and over	17
Role	
Pastor	28
Associate	33
Team Ministry	70
Non-Parish	18
Full-time in Catholic School	23
Not Full-time	35
Implemented RCIA	35
Not Implemented	22

Table C37: RCIA As Best Hope for the Future

	Respondents	
	Bishops Agreed %	Priests Agreed %
Region		
New England	67	
Mideast	70	
Great Lakes	93	
Plains	63	
Southeast	81	
West	83	
Implemented RCIA		67
Not Implemented		47
Years in Parish With School		
None		65
1 - 5		70
6 - 10		66
11 or more		51
Full-time in Catholic School		52
Never Full-time		65
Moderator of Religious Education		54
Never Moderator		66

Table C38: Priests' Perceptions of Sacramental Preparation Programs As Most Common Form of Adult Education

	Priests Agreed %
Years Ordained	
10 or under	96
11 - 20	86
21 - 30	73
31 - 40	69
41 and over	81
Role	
Pastor	74
Associate	86
Team Ministry	100
Non-Parish	89

Table C39: Family-Centered Programs Offering the Best Hope for the Future

	Respondents	
	Bishops Agreed %	Priests Agreed %
Regions		
New England	58	
Mideast	74	
Great Lakes	63	
Plains	88	
Southeast	69	
West	89	
Years Ordained		
10 and under		79
11 - 20		62
21 - 30		77
31 - 40		89
41 and over		89
Member of Religious Community		87
Not Member		76

Table C40: All Programs Should Move Toward Family-Centered Catechesis

	Respondents	
	Bishops Agreed %	Priests Agreed %
Region		
New England	54	55
Mideast	67	71
Great Lakes	61	66
Plains	68	76
Southeast	55	88
West	86	83
Years Ordained		
10 and under		61
11 - 20		58
21 - 30		72
31 - 40		84
41 and over		92
Role		
Pastor		78
Associate		67
Team Ministry		70
Non-Parish		60
Assignment		
Inner City		72
Urban		77
Suburban		59
Rural		78
Attended Catholic Secondary School		69
Did Not Attend		83

Table C41: Parish Secondary Programs Should Include Retreats

	Respondents	
	Bishops Agreed %	Priests Agreed %
Regions		
New England	75	
Mideast	100	
Great Lakes	95	
Plains	88	
Southeast	100	
West	98	
Implemented RCIA		94
Not Implemented		85

Table C42: Parish Programs Should Begin in Preschool

	Respondents	
	Bishops Agreed %	Priests Agreed %
Full-time in Catholic School	90	
Never Full-time	75	
Implemented RCIA	88	
Not Implemented	63	
Regions		
New England		58
Mideast		76
Great Lakes		86
Plains		77
Southeast		88
West		81

Table C43: Priests' Perception that Sacramental Preparation Should Be Unified for All Children and Youth

	Priests Agreed %
Moderator of Religious Education	75
Never Moderator	65
Implemented RCIA	76
Not Implemented	66

Table C44: A Separate Children's Liturgy of the World Should Be Available in Every Parish

	Respondents	
	Bishops Agreed %	Priests Agreed %
Age		
35 and under		68
36 - 45		60
46 - 55		55
56 - 65		43
65 and over		48
Regions		
New England		65
Mideast		58
Great Lakes		49
Plains		26
Southeast		56
West		62
Assignment		
Pastor		49
Associate		67
Team Ministry		54
Non-Parish		43
Years in Parish With School		
None		78
1 - 5		59
6 - 10		48
11 or more		47
Member of Religious Community		64
Not Member		49
Implemented RCIA	55	56
Not Implemented	33	44

REFERENCES

Code of canon law. (1983). Washington, D.C.: Canon Law Society of America.

Greeley, A. M. (1985). *American Catholics since the council: an unauthorized report.* Chicago: Thomas More.

Hinkle, D. E., & Oliver, J. D. (1983). How large should the sample be? A question with no simple answer. *Educational and Psychological Measurement*, 43, pp. 1051-1059.

Kelly, F. D., Benson, P. L., & Donahue, M. J. (1986). *Toward effective parish religious education for children and young people.* Washington, D.C.: National Catholic Educational Association.

Mahoney, J. S. (1987). *Effective and faithful: catechetical ministry in the United States: a study of the studies.* A report to the Department of Education of the United States Catholic Conference, Washington, D.C.

O'Brien, J. S. (Ed.). (1987a). *A primer on educational governance in the Catholic church.* Washington, D.C.: National Catholic Educational Association.

O'Brien, J. S. (1987b). *Mixed messages: what bishops and priests say about Catholic schools.* Washington, D.C.: National Catholic Educational Association.

Sharing the light of faith: national catechetical directory for Catholics of the United States. (1979). Washington, D.C.: United States Catholic Conference.

Thompson, A. D., & Hemrick, E. F. (1982). *The last fifteen years: a statistical survey of Catholic elementary and secondary formal religious education 1965-1980.* Washington, D.C.: United States Catholic Conference.

ABOUT THE AUTHOR

J. Stephen O'Brien is the Executive Director of the Department of Chief Administrators of Catholic Education (CACE) for the National Catholic Educational Association (NCEA). He holds the following degrees: S.T.L. from St. Mary's Seminary and University at Baltimore (1965); M.Ed. in the Teaching of English from the University of Virginia at Charlottesville (1968); M.Ed. in Educational Administration from Virginia Commonwealth University at Richmond (1972); Ed.D. from Virginia Polytechnic Institute and State University at Blacksburg (1987).

A priest of the Diocese of Richmond, Virginia, he has served as teacher and administrator in that diocese, including the position of superintendent of schools and director of Christian education. For seven years he was rector of the cathedral. He has written and edited various books and articles in education and religious education.